DEATH VALLEY TRIVIA

DON LAGO

RIVERBEND
PUBLISHING

ACKNOWLEDGMENTS

Thanks to Janet Spencer for shepherding this book; to Stewart Aitchison for sharing with me his Death Valley explorations; to Death Valley National Park rangers Bob and Lori Spoelhof, Alan Van Valkenberg, Charlie Callagan, Jay Snow, Glenn Johnson, and Dianne Millard for their knowledge and stewardship; to Blair Davenport and Emily Pronovost of the park archives; to Richard Wagner of the Borax Museum for his deep knowledge of mining history; to Chris Langley of the Beverly and Jim Rogers Museum of Lone Pine Film History; and to the Timbisha Shoshone tribe.

Death Valley Trivia
Copyright © 2010 by Don Lago
Published by Riverbend Publishing, Helena, Montana

ISBN 13: 978-1-60639-015-3

Printed in the United States of America.

1 2 3 4 5 6 7 8 9 SB 15 14 13 12 11 10

Cover design by Bob Smith
Text design by Barbara Fifer

Riverbend Publishing
P.O. Box 5833
Helena, MT 59604
1-866-787-2363
www.riverbendpublishing.com

CONTENTS

Geography

How low can you get?

Q. For most people who haven't visited Death Valley National Park, their image of it is only a wide, gray, barren valley. Yet Death Valley is full of surprises, landscapes that might make you think you were in other national parks. These surprises keep people coming back to Death Valley for years. On the following list, there is only one thing that is *not* found in Death Valley. See if you can pick it out:

    1) Slot canyons (just like in Canyonlands National Park)
    2) Sand dunes (just like in Great Sand Dunes National Park)
    3) Colorful badlands (just like in Badlands National Park)
    4) Rocks as old as the oldest rocks at the bottom of the
Grand Canyon

5) Mountains capped with snow into June

6) A valley floor full of cactus and Joshua trees

7) Wild West ghost towns

8) 1,000-pound (453 kg) rocks that move mysteriously

9) Unearthly landscapes where some of *Star Wars* was filmed

10) Wildflower blooms that fill the desert with color

11) A Spanish castle fit for a king

A. 6) A valley floor full of cactus and Joshua trees. Death Valley is too hot and dry and salty even for them. You have to go 600 feet (183 m) above the valley floor before you start to find cactus, and most cactus is above 2,000 feet (609 m). Though Death Valley is only 100 miles (161 km) from Joshua Tree National

---

Death Valley is part of three larger geographic areas, and in each of them, Death Valley is extreme.

The Mojave Desert. There are four deserts in the American Southwest: the Sonoran, the Chihauhuan, the Great Basin, and the Mojave. In summer, the Mojave is the driest desert. Death Valley is the driest and hottest part of the Mojave Desert.

The Great Basin. The Great Basin is a region between the Rocky Mountains and the Sierras where water finds no outlet to the sea. Instead, rivers empty into lakes, where water evaporates. The largest such lake is Utah's Great Salt Lake, which, just like Death Valley, is full of salt. But unlike Death Valley, the Great Salt Lake, which is 4,200 feet (1,280 m) above sea level, has lots of water. Death Valley is the destination lake for the Amargosa River, but with so little rain in the area, the Amargosa River seldom delivers water into Death Valley.

Basin and Range. The Basin and Range province includes most of the Great Basin, plus southern Arizona and New Mexico. In the Basin and Range province, Earth's crust has been stretched apart, creating a series of north-south mountain ranges, with basins in between. Death Valley is in the youngest part of the Basin and Range province, where the mountains are sharper, the valleys deeper. Death Valley is so deep, it's below sea level.

Death Valley is one of 8 national parks in California...

Park, and both parks are part of the Mojave Desert, Death Valley National Park has only a few small, remote areas of Joshua trees. Even by the standards of the Mojave Desert, Death Valley is an extreme environment.

Q. Which of the following statements are true?
A) Death Valley is the driest spot in the U.S.
B) Death Valley is the lowest spot in the Western Hemisphere
C) Death Valley is the hottest spot on Earth
D) All of the above
A. D) All of the above

Q. How big is Death Valley?
A. Death Valley is 130-140 miles (209-225 km) long, though the exact length is hard to define, since the valley gradually tapers off. The valley floor averages about 5 miles (0.8 km) wide, but if you measure from the mountaintops, Death Valley is 15-20 miles wide (24-32 km).

Q. How much of Death Valley is below sea level?

A. Approximately 290 square miles (751 sq km). The area below sea level is 72 miles (116 km) long, about half the length of Death Valley. It is as wide as 7.5 miles (12 km) and as narrow as 0.5 mile (0.8 km). Less than half of this 290 square miles consists of the salt pan, the flat, white areas made of salt deposits.

> "His experienced desert eyes calculated the distance. But this was Death Valley. No traveler of the desert has ever correctly measured distance in this valley of shadows and hazes and illusions. He was making three miles an hour. Yet at the end of an hour he seemed just as far away as ever. Another hour was full of deceits and misjudgments."
> —Zane Grey, *Wanderer of the Wasteland*

Q. True or false: Death Valley makes up less than half of Death Valley National Park.

...California and Alaska are tied for having the most national parks.

A. True. Death Valley is the valley between the Panamint Range and the Amargosa Range. But Death Valley National Park contains a lot of terrain outside of Death Valley itself, including other, smaller valleys, such as Greenwater Valley, Eureka Valley, and Racetrack Valley.

> "One fellow said he knew this was the Creator's dumping place where he had left the worthless dregs after making a world, and the devil had scraped these together a little. Another said this must be the very place where Lot's wife was turned into a pillar of salt, and the pillar been broken up and spread around the country. He said if a man was to die he would never decay on account of the salt."
> —William Manly, *Death Valley 49er*

Q. How did Death Valley get its name?
A. The most common story is that it was named by the 49ers, a group of 1849 Gold Rush pioneers who were looking for a short cut but who found themselves trapped in Death Valley. Their survival ordeal became one of the legends of the Wild West. As one group of pioneers finally crested the mountains and escaped the valley, Juliet Brier looked back and declared, "Goodbye, Death Valley!" But you might be surprised to hear that historians are still debating this and other questions about Death Valley history. The name "Death Valley" didn't appear in print until 1861, a dozen years after the 49ers, enough time for the truth to become vague. Such mysteries and debates help to make history fun.

> Starting with its own name, Death Valley has inspired a lot of grim place names. There's the Funeral Mountains, Coffin Canyon, Hades Canyon, Hells Gate, Devils Hole, Devils Golf Course, Devils Corn Field, Dead Man Pass, Dead Horse Canyon, Suicide Pass, Chaos Ridge, and Dripping Blood Cliffs.

Q. True or false: The auditorium at the park visitor center, where rangers present their evening programs, was designed in the shape of a 1800s coffin, tapering to the foot end.

2.5% of Death Valley National Park is in Nevada, making it one of three national parks to lie…

A. True. And the curtains are black.

Q. Death Valley National Park is the largest national park outside of Alaska. It has nearly 3.4 million acres (3,396,000 acres, to be exact) or 5,306 square miles (13,742 sq km). The next-largest national park outside of Alaska is Yellowstone. How much larger is Death Valley National Park than Yellowstone?

    A) 20 percent   B) 35 percent   C) 50 percent

A. C) Death Valley National Park is over 50 percent larger than Yellowstone's 2.2 million acres (0.89 million ha). In fact, Death Valley National Park is larger than Yellowstone and Yosemite combined. You could fit 4.4 Yosemites inside Death Valley National Park, and 10.9 Grand Tetons. But Alaska has three national parks larger than Death Valley, including the largest of all national parks, Wrangell-St. Elias, at 8.3 million acres (3.36 million ha).

Q. The state of Rhode Island could fit inside Death Valley National Park several times. How many times?

    A) 1.4   B) 2.4   C) 3.4

A. C) 3.4. The state of Rhode Island is 1,545 square miles (4,001 sq km), compared with Death Valley's 5,306 square miles (13,742 sq km). Death Valley National Park is twice the size of Delaware, and nearly the same size as Connecticut.

Q. One of the most important factors in determining the warmth of a place is latitude—your location on the north-south scale. The latitude of Death Valley is equal to the latitude of:

    A) Phoenix   B) Miami   C) Southern Colorado

A. C) Southern Colorado. Death Valley is also at the same latitude as southern Virginia and southern Missouri. It is 700 miles (1,126 km) north of the latitude of Miami. Surprised? There's a lot more than latitude at work in making Death Valley so hot. There's other factors, such as altitude—your distance above sea level.

Q. But Miami is located at sea level, not much higher than Death Valley. If altitude is so important, shouldn't Miami be as hot as Death Valley?

A. In addition to latitude and altitude, there are other factors,

---

...in more than one state. The others are Yellowstone and Great Smoky Mountains.

such as climate. Miami sits on the ocean, with plenty of moisture, while Death Valley sits in the Mojave Desert, which in the summer is the driest desert in North America. In the next chapter, we'll go into more detail about why Death Valley is so dry and so hot.

Q. The U. S. Geological Survey is in charge of making maps of the entire United States. As they survey, they install "bench marks," brass markers that record a location and altitude. These brass markers are pre-manufactured, and all a surveyor needs to do is to chisel in some numbers, such as for altitude. But these brass markers weren't made with Death Valley in mind. Surveyors in Death Valley needed to scratch out one phrase on the markers. What was it?
A. "Above Sea Level." You can see one of these markers, with "Above Sea Level" scratched out, behind the Borax Museum at Furnace Creek Ranch.

Q. How far below sea level is Death Valley?
   A) 102 feet (31 m)   B) 182 feet (55 m)   C) 282 feet (86 m)
A. C) 282 feet (86 m), at Badwater. Actually, near the Badwater parking area you are 279 feet (85 m) below sea level. You'd have to go several miles out onto the salt pan to find a few dips that are 282 feet (86 m) below sea level.

Q. Death Valley is the lowest spot in the Western Hemisphere (North and South America). What's the lowest spot in the world?
A. The Dead Sea (between Jordan and Israel) is 1,360 feet (414 m) below sea level.

Q. How many places on Earth are deeper than Death Valley?
   A) 2   B) 6   C) 15
A. B) Only six. Three are in East Africa: one in Egypt at -435 feet (-132 m); one in Ethiopia at -410 feet (-125 m); and one in Djibouti at -509 feet (-155 m). Three are in Asia: one in Kazakhstan at -433 feet (-132 m); one in China at -505 feet (-154 m); and the Dead Sea at -1,360 feet (-414 m).

Q. All of the places listed above are in deserts. Can you think of any

---

The hand-made relief map in the park visitor center
took 2,000 hours of work.

reason why deserts are associated with areas below sea level?

A. If these valleys received more rain, erosion would fill them up with sediments and they would no longer be below sea level. Also, they'd be full of water and be lakes, not valleys.

Q. All of the places listed above were created by the same force. What?

   A) Rivers   B) Meteorite impacts   C) Plate tectonics

A. C) Plate tectonics. Earth's crust is made of large sections, or plates, that are slowly pushed about by the currents of magma welling up from inside the planet. In some places tectonic plates collide and form mountain ranges, and in other places they pull apart and allow blocks of crust to drop down, even drop below sea level. See more about plate tectonics in the geology chapter.

Q. Who first discovered that Death Valley was below sea level?

A. In 1861 a U. S. survey expedition came into Death Valley. Their guide, Joel Brooks, suggested that Death Valley might be below sea level. Brooks didn't have much credibility, since he wasn't a good guide. But when the surveyors took barometer readings, they discovered that Brooks was right.

Q. True or false: The surveyors who discovered that Death Valley was below sea level were using camels as pack animals.

A. True. In 1856 Jefferson Davis (then the U.S. Secretary of War, and soon the president of the Confederacy) started an experiment in the use of camels in the desert Southwest. He obtained camels and a camel driver from the Middle East. The camels did well on open, sandy terrain, but they hated to climb rugged slopes, which mules handled easily. The 1861 survey brought three camels into Death Valley, but this was the camels' final test. Many years later, prospector Shorty Harris was struggling through the Mojave Desert when he decided he must be hallucinating, for he thought he was seeing a camel. It was one of Jeff Davis's camels, turned loose long ago.

The mountain passes where highways enter Death Valley are all over 3,000 feet (914 m).

Q. Which is farther from sea level: Death Valley (below sea level) or Memphis, Tennessee (above sea level)?
A. Memphis is 254 feet (77 m) above sea level, so Death Valley, at 282 feet (86 m) below sea level, is 28 feet (8.5 m) farther.

Q. Which is farther from sea level: Death Valley, or the highest point in Florida?
A. The highest point in Florida is 345 feet (105 m) above sea level, only 63 feet (19 m) farther from sea level than Death Valley.

Q. If Lake Erie was placed inside Death Valley, would it fill Death Valley up to sea level?
A. No. Lake Erie is 210 feet (64 m) deep at its deepest spot. In Death Valley, Lake Erie would still be 72 feet (22 m) below sea level. Hudson Bay, with an average depth of 305 feet (93 m), would barely fill Death Valley to sea level.

Q. Which is deeper below sea level: the bottom of the English Channel, or Death Valley?
A. The English Channel is 190 feet (59 m) deep, 92 feet (28 m) shallower than Death Valley.

Q. If Niagara Falls started at sea level above Badwater, would its length reach the valley floor?
A. No. Niagara Falls is 182 feet (55 m) tall, so it would have to fall another 100 feet (30 m) to reach the floor of Death Valley.

Q. If you placed the Statue of Liberty at the bottom of Death Valley, would its torch reach sea level?
A. Only if you include the statue's stone pedestal. The statue itself is 151 feet (46 m) tall, and with its pedestal it is 305 feet (93 m) tall, so its torch would stick out 23 feet (7 m) above sea level. London's Big Ben is 315 feet (96 m) tall, so its spire—but not its clock—would stick out. The Sydney Opera House is 220 feet (67 m) tall, so it

Badwater got its name when a prospector's burro refused to drink its water...

would be 62 feet (19 m) underwater. The U. S. Capitol building is 289 feet (88 m) tall, so it would stick out five feet above water.

Q. When the *Titanic* sank, it fell to a depth of 12,460 feet (3,797 m), slightly deeper than the Atlantic Ocean's average depth of 12,254 feet (3,735 m). When you are standing at Badwater, what percent of the way are you to the depth of the *Titanic*?
   A) 0.5 percent   B) 1.5 percent   C) 2.2 percent
A. C) 2.2 percent, or 1/44th the depth of the *Titanic*. You are well below the 100-foot (30 m) depth at which coral reefs can grow. You are at about 40 percent of the depth to where light can no longer penetrate the sea enough to support plants. You are at about 10 percent of the depth at which sperm whales swim.

Q. What's the highest point in Death Valley National Park?
A. Telescope Peak, at 11,049 feet (3,367 m). Named for its great views, Telescope Peak is higher than the highest points in 37 states. Tele-

Telescope Peak

scope Peak is directly across the valley from Badwater, making a total elevation difference of 11,331 feet (3,453 m). Nowhere else in the United States does such a large elevation difference occur in such a short distance. Telescope Peak towers two miles above Badwater—equal to twice the depth of the Grand Canyon.

Q. The highest spot in the continental United States, California's Mt. Whitney, at 14,491 feet (4,416 m), is only 85 miles (137 km) from the lowest spot, Death Valley. Is it just a coincidence that the highest spot and the lowest spot are so close?
A. No, both were created by the tectonic forces that created the Basin and Range province. In the Basin and Range, Earth's crust is stretching apart, causing a series of mountain ranges and deep valleys. These tectonic forces are more dynamic in southern California than anywhere else. We'll talk more about the Basin and Range in the geology chapter.

...The pool at Badwater is 7 percent salt, the same as sea water.

Q. Can you see Mt. Whitney from Badwater?
A. No, the view is blocked by the Panamint Mountains. In fact, you can't even see Mt. Whitney from Dantes View, which is 5,475 feet (1,669 m) high, directly behind Badwater.

Q. If you started filling Death Valley with water, how high would the water need to get before it overflowed the valley?
A) 282 feet (86 m)   B) 600 feet (183 m)   C) 2,000 feet (609 m)
A. B) 600 feet (183 m). Water would overflow at the southern end of Death Valley, where the Amargosa River flows in. During the Ice Age about 100,000 years ago, lots of water was flowing into Death Valley, forming a lake 600 feet (183 m) deep.

Q. If you continued filling Death Valley with water until it over-flowed and filled up the whole southern California Basin and Range country, how high would the water need to get before it found an outlet to the sea?'
A) 600 feet (183 m)   B) 2,000 feet (609 m)
C) 4,000 feet (1,219 m)
A. B) 2,000 feet (609 m). Then it would drain into the Colorado River.

Q. The 600-foot (183 m) deep lake that filled Death Valley dur-ing the Ice Age, Lake Manly, was about 90 miles (145 km) long and 8 miles (12.8 km) wide. If you were to place the Washington Monument in Lake Manly, would it stick out?
A. No, the Washington Monu-ment is only 555 feet (169 m) tall. Seattle's Space Needle, at 605 feet (184 m), might still be submerged, but the St. Louis Gateway Arch, at 630 feet (189 m), would stick out.

Q. The best place to see evidence of Lake Manly is Shoreline

Titus Canyon was named for Edgar Titus, a prospector
who disappeared there...

Butte, at the southern end of Death Valley. What marks did Lake Manly leave on Shoreline Butte?

A. Shorelines! Think about a beach at the ocean: the constant pounding of waves carves out a sloping shore. As the level of Lake Manly dropped over thousands of years, waves carved out a series of shorelines, like a stairway. There are other places in Death Valley where you can see "fossil" shorelines, including on the cliffs right behind Badwater, but these are trickier to spot.

Q. About 2,000 years ago, when the climate was temporarily wetter, there was another lake in Death Valley, about 30 feet (9 m) deep. We know it was 30 feet (9 m) deep because something left a "bathtub ring" of rocks at that level. These rocks were arranged into many small circles. What created these rock circles?

   A) Waves   B) Wind   C) Native Americans

A. C) Native Americans. These rock circles were their campfires, built near the shoreline.

Q. Death Valley has over 350 seeps and springs. Some are barely large enough to keep the ground damp, but the largest, Travertine Spring, can pour out up to 2,000 gallons (7,580 L) per minute. Springs supply all the water needs of park residents and tourists. Naturally warm spring water replaces the water in the swimming pool at Furnace Creek Inn five times a day (so the pool requires no chlorine), and is then used to water lawns and trees. If Death Valley wasn't so dry, its springs would start building a lake on the valley floor. Where does all this water come from?

   A) The mountains of central Nevada, hundreds of miles away
   B) The Sierras, 75 miles (120 km) away
   C) The Colorado River, leaking underground

A. A) The mountains of central Nevada. Snowmelt flows underground for hundreds of miles until water reaches the surface on the east side of Death Valley. Of course, in Death Valley the surface dives down to meet the water; underground water would have to be more than 282 feet (86 m) below sea level to avoid coming out at Badwater. This water can take thousands of years to arrive in Death Valley. This means that the tap water you are drinking in Death Valley may have fallen as rain when the Egyptian pyramids were being built.

...in the summer of 1905. He probably died of the heat.

Q. True or false: There is no place in Death Valley more than 15 miles (24 km) away from a spring.
A. True. Native Americans knew all the water sources in Death Valley. But prospectors and tourists have died of thirst even when springs were nearby.

Q. True or false: The Panamint Mountains were named by prospectors who went there to "pan a mint."
A. False. "Panumunt" was the name the Southern Paiutes gave to the tribe that lived in Death Valley.

Place names in Death Valley have interesting origins. Furnace Creek was named not for the heat, but because an early explorer, Dr. Darwin French, reported seeing an old miner's furnace there. Dr. French gave his own first name to Darwin Falls and the town of Darwin. Many features were named for 49ers, such as Manly Beacon and Lake Manly, or for later miners, such as Aguerreberry Point. Zabriskie Point and Gower Gulch were named for Borax Company executives. (The Borax Company has had several names over the decades, so to avoid confusion this book will call it simply "the Borax Company"). Dead Man Pass was named for an unknown dead man found there. Some names got garbled: Daylight Pass was originally "Delight Pass," and Wingate Pass was originally "Windy Gate." "Amargosa" is the Spanish word for "bitter," describing the water in the Amargosa River. Some Native American place names have endured: Ubehebe means "big basket in the rocks."

Q. Death Valley National Park gets about one million visitors per year. What's the busiest season for visitation?
   A) Winter   B) Spring   C) Summer   D) Fall
A. Spring. (Since spring and summer start earlier in Death Valley than elsewhere, and since the National Park Service counts visitors by month and not by season, we are defining spring as the months of March, April, and May). Fall (September, October, and November) is the second busiest season. Surprisingly, summer (June, July, and August) is almost always busier than winter

---

The Amargosa River drains an area of 6,000 square miles
(15,539 sq km).

(December, January, and February). In the 14 years between when Death Valley became a national park in 1994 (before that, it was a national monument) and 2007, there was only one year when summer visitation was less than winter visitation. Here are the actual average numbers: Spring: 285,000; Fall: 260,000; Summer: 245,000; Winter: 192,000.

Q. Has summer ever been the busiest season at Death Valley National Park?
A. In the 14 years between 1994 and 2007, summer was the busiest season twice, but just barely. August was the busiest month three times, and the second busiest month twice. Some people are curious to experience 120 F (49 C) heat.

Q. Which month is most often the busiest month at Death Valley National Park?
   A) March   B) April   C) May
A. B) April. In the 14 years between 1994 and 2007, April was the busiest month five times, and the second busiest month five times. March was the busiest month four times. The least busy month is usually December.

Q. Here's an odd statistic: The slowest two months for visitation since Death Valley became a national park were December 2004, and January 2005, each with about 26,000 visitors. But two months later Death Valley had one of its busiest months ever: 128,000 visitors. What was going on?
A. In August 2004, heavy rainstorms caused flash floods that tore up the highways and closed many of the facilities and attractions in

Desertgold blooming the in park

Death Valley. But those same rains triggered a spectacular spring wildflower bloom, which received national media attention and brought people flocking to the park.

In summer, over 90 percent of Death Valley visitors are Europeans.

Q. The Wilderness Act of 1964 provided that areas be preserved as nature made them, as homes for wildlife, not for human uses, not even for roads. What percentage of Death Valley National Park is designated as wilderness?
  A) 10 percent   B) 50 percent   C) 95 percent
A. C) 95 percent.

Q. Death Valley has far fewer human-made hiking trails than many national parks. Why is this?
A. Building a trail usually means clearing a route through forests, and Death Valley doesn't have many forests. But there's plenty of great hiking in nature-made routes—canyons.

Q. Death Valley is one of the best national parks for which activity?
  A) Bird watching   B) Star gazing   C) Rock climbing
A. B) Star gazing. Death Valley has some of the darkest skies of any national park. It's a long way from city lights, and almost never has clouds or even humidity. The view of the Milky Way can be spectacular. Park rangers and amateur astronomers regularly set up telescopes for public viewings.

Q. True or false: Scuba divers make regular visits to Death Valley to go diving.
A. True. They are actually National Park Service biologists who dive into the Devils Hole under-water cave, the home of the pupfish, an endangered species. The divers dive there every two or three months to count the pupfish population, which has sometimes been dangerously low.

Q. The book store in the park visitor center is run by the Death Valley Natural History Association. What is this?
A. Most national parks have a "cooperating association" that is responsible for selling educational items to the public. This idea started in Yosemite in 1923. The National Park Service (NPS) was

---

Cow Creek, which today holds Park Service housing and offices...

a new agency with a small budget and lots of needs, but the NPS was prohibited from raising money directly from the public. Lovers of Yosemite got together to raise money to help the NPS build a museum. By the year 2000 there were 65 cooperating associations, which raised $112 million annually, donated $26 million directly to the NPS, and used millions more for their own educational programs and publications. The Death Valley Natural History Association was founded in 1954 and soon published its first book, *The Borax Story.* By 2004, the 50th anniversary of its founding, the Death Valley Natural History Association had donated over $2 million to Death Valley National Park.

"Why should the lovely things of the earth—the grasses, the trees, the lakes, the little hills—appear trivial and insignificant when we come face to face with the sea or the desert or the vastness of the midnight sky?...They are the great elements. We do not see, we hardly know if their boundaries are limited; we only feel their immensity, their mystery, and their beauty."

—John C. Van Dyke, *The Desert*

...was originally the ranch of M. M. Beatty, for whom Beatty, Nevada, was named.

WEATHER
THE HEAT IS ON

Q. What was the hottest temperature ever recorded in Death Valley?

A) 125 F (51.6 C)   B) 128 F (53 C)   C) 134 F (56.6 C)

A. C) 134 F (56.6 C). It was recorded on July 13, 1913, at Furnace Creek Ranch.

"On the day I recorded the greatest heat ever registered—134 in the shade—I thought the world was going to come to an end. Swallows in full flight fell to the ground dead, and when I went out to read the thermometer with a wet Turkish towel on my head, it was dry before I returned."

—Oscar Denton

Q. Was Death Valley's record 134 F (56.6 C) the hottest temperature ever recorded on Earth?
A. Almost. In 1922 a temperature of 136 F (57.7 C) was recorded
in the Sahara Desert in Libya. But when it comes to average highs,
Death Valley beats the Sahara. Death Valley is the hottest place
on Earth. In fact, Death Valley's 1913 high temperature might
have beaten the Saraha's 136 F (57.7 C) if it had been recorded
at Badwater, which is usually hotter than Furnace Creek Ranch.
Death Valley's 134 F (56.6 C) beat Europe's record high of 117 F
(47 C) by 17 degrees F (10 degrees C). It beat Australia's record
high of 123 F (50.5 C) by 11 degrees F (6.1 degrees C). It beat
the Dead Sea's record high of 129 F (53.8 C) by 5 degrees F (2.8
degrees C).

Q. How many days in a row has Death Valley hit 100 F (37.8 C)
or higher?
    A) 34   B) 99   C) 154
A. C) 154 days in a row, in 2001. That's over five months.

Q. In how many months of the year has Death Valley hit 100 F
(37.8 C) or higher?
    A) 6   B) 7   C) 8
A. C) 8. Only four months, (November, December, January, and
February), have never recorded a 100 F (37.8 C) day. Even March
has hit 102 F (38.8 C). From June to September, the *average* daily
high is over 100 F (37.8 C). In May the average daily high is 99 F
(37.2 C).

Q. How many days in a row has Death Valley hit 110 F (43 C) or
higher?
    A) 87   B) 99   C) 110
A. C) 110 days in a row, in 1996.

Q. How many days in a row has Death Valley hit 120 F (49 C) or
higher?
    A) 5   B) 43   C) 52
A. B) 43 days in a row, in 1917. In all, 1917 saw 52 days over
120 F (49 C).

Death Valley has fewer cloudy days than anywhere else in the U.S.

Q. True or false: Every year since weather records have been kept in Death Valley, highs have hit 120 F (49 C) at least one day.
A. True. And half of those years, highs have hit 125 F (51.6 C).

Q. How many days in a row has Death Valley hit 129 F (53.8 C) or higher?
   A) 4   B) 5   C) 10
A. B) 5 days. This was in 1913, and one of those days was the record 134 F (56.6 C).

Q. What's the hottest month in Death Valley?
   A) June   B) July   C) August
A. B) July. The average daily high is 115 F (46 C). August is second, with an average daily high of 113 F (45C). June is third, at 109 F (42.7 C).

Q. In July, when the average daily high is 115 F (46 C), what's the average daily low?
A) 68 F (20 C)   B) 78 F (25.5 C)
C) 88 F (31 C)
A. C) 88 F (31 C). Yes, that's the *low*. The difference between July's average high and average low is 27 degrees F (15 degrees C), which is one of the smallest differences of the year. In July, nights are slow to cool down. In August the average daily low is 85 F (29.4 C), and in June it's 80 F (26.7 C).

Q. For how many months of the year is Death Valley's average daily high below 80 F (26.6 C)?
   A) 4   B) 5   C) 6
A. A) 4. In November the average daily high is 76 F (24.4 C), in February it's 72 F (22.2 C), and in January and December it's 65 F (18.3 C).

Q. By how many degrees did Death Valley's record temperature of 134 F (56.6 C) beat the hottest temperature ever recorded in Dallas, Texas?
   A) 15 F (8.3 C)   B) 25 F (13.9 C)   C) 40 F (22 C)
A. B) 25 F (13.9 C). The hottest day ever recorded in Dallas was

---

*A desert is defined as a place that gets less than 10 inches (25 cm)
of rain per year.*

109 F (42.7 C), 25 degrees F (13.9 degrees C) cooler than Death Valley's 134 (56.6 C). And Death Valley beat Anchorage, Alaska, whose record high was 85 F (29 C) degrees, by 49 degrees F (27 degrees C).

Q. Death Valley's official temperature is recorded at a weather station five feet (1.5 m) above the ground. But the ground gets hotter than the air. What's the hottest ground temperature ever recorded in Death Valley?
    A) 150 F (66 C)   B) 175 F (80 C)   C) 201 F (93.8 C)
A. C) 201 F (93.8 C), in 1972.

Q. True or false: You can fry eggs on the sidewalk in a Death Valley summer.
A. True. To cook fully, an egg needs to be 158 F (70 C). With a temperature near 200 F (93 C), Death's Valley's ground could actually burn an egg. It depends on whether you use a light-colored concrete sidewalk, which absorbs about 50 percent of the sun's energy, or black asphalt, which absorbs about 90 percent of the sun's energy. But Death Valley's rangers have gotten tired of trying to clean fried eggs off the sidewalk, so they suggest that you fry your eggs on the hood of your car. If you want toast to go with your eggs, just take fresh bread and hold it in the air for a minute.

> "It has all the advantages of hell without the inconveniences."
> —a Death Valley newspaper, 1907

Q. If you think Death Valley is hot in summer, be glad you don't have the job of Fred Corkill, who ran the assay laboratory at the Ryan borax mine. In July of 1913, when Death Valley was setting its 134 F (56.6 C) record, what did the thermometer say in Fred's lab?
    A) 149 F (65 C)   B) 159 F (70.5 C)   C) 173 F (78 C)
A. C) 173 F (78 C)

The Mojave Desert is only about 10,000 to 12,000 years old...

In the summer of 1891 the U.S. Weather Bureau established its first weather station in Death Valley, but the weatherman quit after a few months, declaring that he would rather "take Hell straight" than take any more of Death Valley.

Q. What's the record low temperature in Death Valley?
    A) -12 F (-24 C)   B) 0 F (-17.8 C)   C) 15 F (-10 C)
A. C) 15 F (-10 C), in 1913, which was the same year that set the record high of 134 F (56.6 C). Death Valley's all-time low is about the same as the all-time lows of Phoenix, Arizona, and Houston, Texas.

Q. True or false: Death Valley's record low of 15 F (-10 C) is warmer than the record lows of all 50 states.
A. True. Even Hawaii's record low is a few degrees cooler than Death Valley's record low. Death Valley simply doesn't get very cold. Every state except Hawaii—even Florida—has had record lows below 0 F (-17.8 C). Forty-eight states have had record lows below -10 F (-23 C). Thirty-eight states have had record lows below -30 F (-34 C). Sixteen states have had record lows below -50 F (-46 C). Alaska's record low was -80 F (-62 C). Of course, when we talk about Death Valley's record low, we are talking about the valley floor; if you included the mountains, it would be a lot cooler.

Q. The difference between Death Valley's record high and its record low is 119 F (66.6 C). If you compared this temperature spread with the spread of record highs and record lows in each of the 50 states, Death Valley would rank near the far end of the ranking. Which end?
    A) Death Valley's temperature spread is greater than 49
    states.
    B) Death Valley's temperature spread is smaller than 49
    states.
A. B) Only Hawaii has a smaller temperature spread than Death Valley, with a 112 F (63 C) difference between its record high and record low. The state with the largest spread between its record high and record low is Montana, with a difference of 187 F (103 C).

...it formed at the end of the last Ice Age.

Q. What's the record low temperature for August in Death Valley?
  A) 32 F (0 C)   B) 42 F (5.5 C)   C) 64 F (18 C)
A. C) 64 F (18 C) is as cool as it's ever been in August. Even July, the hottest month on average, has gotten down to 52 F (11 C).

Q. The coolest months in Death Valley are December and January, with their average daily high of 65 F (18 C). These are the only two months that have never hit 90 F (32 C). What is the average daily low in December and January?
  A) 25 F (-4 C)   B) 32 F (0 C)   C) 39 F (4 C)
A. C) 39 F (4 C). These are the only two months when the average low is below 40 F (4.4 C).

Q. In addition to its extreme heat, Death Valley is famous for its extreme dryness. True or false: In some years, Death Valley has recorded no rainfall.
A. True. In 1929 and 1953, no rainfall at all was recorded in Death Valley.

Q. What's the average annual rainfall in Death Valley?
  A) 1.94 inches (4.9 cm)   B) 2.94 inches (7.5 cm)
  C) 5.94 inches (15 cm)
A. A) Only 1.94 inches (4.9 cm). To visualize this amount, imagine a soda can, a bit less than five inches (13 cm) tall. Death Valley's annual rainfall wouldn't fill a soda can even half full.

Q. The driest period ever recorded in Death Valley was a 40-month period in 1931-34, the Dust Bowl years in the American Midwest. How much total rain fell?
  A) 0.64 inch (1.6 cm)   B) 1.94 inches (4.9 cm)
  C) 3.2 inches (8.1 cm)
A. A) 0.64 inch (1.6 cm). That's a rate of 0.19 inch (0.5 cm) per year.

Q. The wettest spot on Earth is a town in India called Mawsynram. How many times more rain does it get than Death Valley?
  A) 100 times more   B) 147 times more   C) 241 times more
A. C) 241 times more. Mawsynram gets 467.4 inches (11.87 m)

Some car rental companies forbid customers from taking cars into Death Valley in summer...

of rain per year. It would take Death Valley 241 years to equal one year of rain in Mawsynram.

Q. Compared with Death Valley, how many times more annual rainfall does Phoenix, Arizona, receive?

A) Twice as muchB) 4.3 times more
C) 7.1 times more

A. B) 4.3 times more. Phoenix receives an average of 8.29 inches (21 cm) of rain per year. In its wettest year ever, 2005, when Death Valley received 4.73 inches (12 cm) of rain, this was still barely half of Phoenix's average.

Q. Compared with Death Valley, how many times more annual rainfall does New York City receive?

A) 16 times more   B) 20 times more   C) 26 times more

A. C) 26 times more. New York City receives an average of 49.64 inches (126 cm) of rain per year. New Orleans, with an average of 64.16 inches (163 cm) of rain per year, receives 33 times more rain than Death Valley.

> Joke: In Death Valley, a "five inch rain" is a rain that leaves five inches (13 cm) between rain drops.

Q. Which month is the driest month in Death Valley?

A) May   B) June   C) July

A. B) June has the least rainfall, an average of 0.04 inch (0.1 cm). May is the second driest with 0.08 inch (0.2 cm).

Q. Which month is the wettest month in Death Valley?

A) April   B) February   C) November

A. B) February has the most rainfall, with an average of 0.35 inch (0.9 cm). January is second with 0.26 inch (0.66 cm). March is third with 0.25 inch (0.63 cm).

Q. The wettest month ever recorded in Death Valley was January, 1995. How much rain fell?

...to avoid engine damage from overheating.

A) 1.56 inches (3.9 cm)   B) 2.1 inches (5.3 cm)
C) 2.59 inches (6.6 cm)
A. C) 2.59 inches (6.6 cm). That's more than the average annual rainfall of 1.94 inches (4.9 cm).

Q. Because Death Valley is so hot, its rate of evaporation is much higher than its rate of precipitation. How many inches of water could evaporate from Death Valley in one year?
A) 25 inches (63 cm)   B) 50 inches (127 cm)
C) 150 inches (381 cm)
A. C) 150 inches (381 cm). That's over 75 times the average annual rainfall in Death Valley. If you put 12 feet (3.65 m) of water on the floor of Death Valley, it would be gone in only one year.

Q. With so little rainfall and so much evaporation, the humidity level in Death Valley is very low. In summers, how low does it get?
A) 2 percent   B) 5 percent   C) 10 percent
A. A) As low as 2 percent. In very humid parts of the U.S. there's an expression about what makes people miserable: "It's not the heat, it's the humidity." In Death Valley, it's often not the heat that kills people, it's the *low* humidity, which rapidly dehydrates them. Even when the temperature is a pleasant 70 F (21 C), people can become seriously dehydrated. You may have also heard the expression "It's a dry heat," which implies that low humidity is a good thing. But in the desert, dryness *kills*.

Q. The floor of Death Valley may receive less than 2 inches (5 cm) of precipitation per year, but the Panamint Mountains (on the west side of the valley) receive more. How much?
A) 5 inches (13 cm) per year   B) 10 inches (25 cm)
C) 15 inches (38 cm)
A. C) 15 inches (38 cm) on the highest peaks. When you turn 15 inches (38 cm) of rain into snow, this amounts to 20 feet (6 m) of snow on Telescope Peak, which is 11,049 feet (3,368 m) high. At the 7,000 foot (2,134 m) level, the Panamints get about 9 inches (23 cm) of precipitation.

Q. How long into the year does the snow on the Panamints last?
A) April   B) May   C) June

Death Valley winds have been clocked at 80 miles (128 km) per hour...

A. C) Patches of snow may last into June. Beyond June, Death Valley snow "doesn't stand a snowball's chance in hell."

Q. True or false: When the snow melts on the Panamints, it creates streams and waterfalls that flow to the bottom of Death Valley.
A. False. Death Valley's evaporation rate is so high that most of the snow disappears straight into the air.

Q. Does it ever snow on the valley floor?
A. Very rarely, and the snow melts fast. But there's a photo of an inch or two (2-5 cm) of snow on the sign at Badwater.

Q. Why is Death Valley so dry?
A. The secret to Death Valley's dryness is the "rain shadow" effect. When storms come out of the Pacific Ocean and head inland, they have to cross a series of mountain ranges, which force clouds to rise, condense, and drop their moisture. The Sierras can get 34 feet (10 m) of snow per year, but then the clouds have little moisture left for the Owens Valley just west of the Sierras; the Owens Valley gets less than 6 inches (15 cm) of rain per year. Clouds that make it past the Sierras then hit the Panamint Mountains and lose most of their remaining moisture. This leaves little rain for Death Valley, or for the Amargosa Range

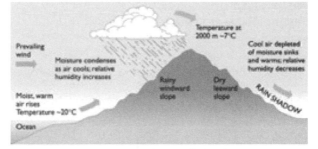

on the east side of Death Valley. While the Panamints get 15 inches (38 cm) of annual precipitation, the Amargosa Range gets only 3-5 inches (7-12 cm). This is why Dantes View, on the crest of the Amargosa Range, is so bare of vegetation. The Basin and Range country, with its series of north-south mountain ranges, is a perfect system for blocking rain and creating deserts.

...and they probably get a lot higher.

Q. Why is Death Valley so hot?
A. It's partly because of its low elevation. As a general rule, with every thousand feet you lose in elevation, the temperature rises by about 5 degrees F (3 degrees C). This means that Badwater is about 25 degrees F (14 degrees C) hotter than Dantes View, and about 50 degrees F (28 degrees C) hotter than Telescope Peak. Death Valley's topography—a deep valley sandwiched between two steep mountain ranges—also magnifies the heat. Hot air rising from the valley floor gets trapped between the mountain ranges. The hot air recirculates, and only gets hotter. The dryness also contributes to the heat. Death Valley has no clouds for shade, no rain for cooling, and little vegetation to stop rocks from absorbing heat all day. In turn, the heat reinforces the dryness, evaporating rain before it can reach the ground. Basin and Range geology, in creating tall mountain ranges to block rainfall and a deep valley to trap heat, has come up with the perfect formula for making Death Valley so hot.

Q. The term "tree line" is an altitude at which trees will no longer grow. This term is usually used for mountains, for altitudes too high and wintry for trees. But in Death Valley this term is used for where it's too low and too hot for trees to grow. At what altitude is this tree line in Death Valley?
A) 2,000 feet (610 m)   B) 4,000 feet (1,219 m)
C) 6,000 feet (1,829 m)
A. C) About 6,000 feet (1,829 m).

Q. How does heat cause mirages?
    A) People suffering from the heat have delusions of seeing water.
    B) The heat bends light rays, creating optical illusions.
A. B) The heat bends light rays, making images waver, creating the illusion of water.

Q. True or false: Even in the summer heat, people in Death Valley may not get sweaty.
A. True. The human skin often remains dry. But this doesn't mean you aren't perspiring: it means that perspiration is evaporating

---

Dust devils look like tornadoes, but aren't nearly as powerful.

instantly. For people from humid climates, who are accustomed to skin and clothes drenched with sweat, this can trick them into seriously underestimating how much water they are losing.

Q. If someone is exercising in 120 F (49 C) heat and 2 percent humidity, how long does it take for them to lose a gallon (3.7 L) of water?

    A) One hour   B) 5 hours   C) 10 hours

A. A) One hour.

Q. If someone is sitting in the shade in 120 F (49 C) heat and 2 percent humidity, how much water can they lose in one day?

A) One gallon (3.8 L)   B) 1.5 gallons (5.7 L)   C) 2 gallons (7.6 L)

A. C) 2 gallons (7.6 L). This is why park rangers urge visitors to drink *at least* one gallon (3.8 L) of water per day.

Q. In hot weather, you can feel a lot cooler by removing your shirt, so why do park rangers warn against doing so?

A. You may *feel* cooler, but it's only because of evaporative cooling—because you are losing lots of moisture from your torso, including from your heart and lungs, which are already overstressed by the heat. When you remove a shirt, or fail to wear a hat, your evaporation rate soars, and so does the danger of heat stroke.

Q. How many people die from the heat in Death Valley every year?

A. Usually at least two, sometimes more.

Q. A person will be dehydrated after losing how much body fluid?

    A) 2.5 percent   B) 5 percent   C) 10 percent

A. A) 2.5 percent. The first warning sign of dehydration is often a lack of energy and a bad mood, then a headache. By 5 percent, a person becomes nauseous. By 10 percent, dizziness and headaches may be incapacitating. By 15 percent, death is imminent.

Rainfall that evaporates before hitting the ground is called "virga."

Q. If you were in Death Valley in the summer heat and saw a bunch of people running down the highway, what are they doing?
  A) Escaped from an insane asylum
  B) Gone insane from the heat
  C) Running a marathon

A. C) It's not just a marathon, it's the Badwater Ultramarathon, which goes 135 miles (217 km) from Badwater to Mt. Whitney, from the lowest point in the U.S. to the highest. Only very experienced and well-trained runners are allowed to enter. They run through 115+ F (45+ C) heat. About two dozen runners participate. Many drop out. The record is about 26 hours, though for most runners it takes more like two days, including time for rest along the way. The heat of the asphalt has caused running shoes to disintegrate. Since human feet swell with heat, some runners use five pairs of shoes, each one a size larger, to complete the race.

Q. Desert animals are tough, but even they need to avoid the sun. How long does it take for a desert tortoise to die if it is exposed to the desert summer sun?
  A) One hour   B) 12 hours   C) 5 days
A. A) One hour. Desert tortoises stay underground to avoid the sun.

Q. People have tried some clever strategies for living in Death Valley's heat. Miners slept in Furnace Creek to stay cool, propping up their heads to avoid drowning. People have put their clothes in refrigerators overnight. Before going to bed, people showered in their nightgowns or underwear. People still wear gloves to avoid burning their hands on car doors. Native Americans simply moved up into the Panamint Mountains in the summer. Until air conditioning arrived, the National Park Service moved its headquarters up to Wildrose, at 4,100 feet (1,250 m) in the Panamints, every summer. But Death Valley does have advantages. How long does it take for laundry hung on a clotheslines to dry?
  A) 2 minutes   B) 5 minutes   C) 10 minutes
A. A) 2 minutes.

"Desert pavement," a ground packed with tight-fitting stones...

Q. How much do Death Valley residents pay for air conditioning in summer?

A) $200 per month   B) $300 per month   C) $400 per month

A. C) $400 per month. But many Death Valley residences have swamp coolers, which use evaporative cooling and cost much less. Another problem in Death Valley is that the ground temperature of nearly 200 F (93 C) makes pipes so hot that tap water becomes too hot to drink. Residents begin using their cold water faucets for hot water, and turn their hot water tanks into reservoirs where water can cool down enough to be used.

Q. Do people camp out or stay in RVs in Death Valley summers?

A. Some try camping out, but usually only for one night. The lows in the summer may be in the upper 80s F (30 C), but this is just before sunrise. At bedtime it may still be 120 F (49 C). Inside a small plastic tent it gets much hotter, so campers try sleeping atop picnic tables. Nor is living in a metal box in 120 F (49 C) heat much fun. In the entire month of August 2006, there were only 6 RVs in Death Valley campgrounds. (By early November, the time of the annual Death Valley 49ers Encampment, there are over 1,000 RVs every night). Most summer visitors stay in the lodges.

Q. Death Valley might seem an unlikely place for flash floods, but in fact flash floods are often worse in Southwestern deserts than elsewhere. Why is this?

    A) The topography funnels rain waters into narrow, steep canyons

    B) The rocky land can't absorb water

    C) There is little vegetation to absorb water

    D) Rain comes in intense thunderstorms

    E) All of the above

A. E) All of the above. In Death Valley the winter rains are usually gentle and steady, but summer brings intense thunderstorms and flash floods. There's a flash flood somewhere in Death Valley almost every year, but in any one place, there might be 20 to 50 years between floods.

...can absorb only 10 percent of the moisture of normal soils.

Q. Titus Canyon drains an area of 35 square miles (90 sq km). All the water that falls into this area has to exit through a canyon that gets as narrow as 15 feet (4.5 m). This means that one inch (2.5 cm) of rain will pile up into a much higher flow as it roars through Titus Canyon. How high can this flood get?

   A) 4 feet (1.2 m)   B) 10 feet (3 m)   C) 20 feet (6 m)

A. C) 20 feet (6 m). As you walk through narrow canyons like Titus, Mosaic, or Golden, you can see evidence of past flash floods: mud stains high on canyon walls, rocks perched on ledges, and undercut banks of dirt.

Q. True or false: In the summer you can see snowplows at work on the roads of Death Valley.

A. True. The National Park Service uses snowplows and street sweepers to clear the roads of debris after flash floods.

Q. On August 15, 2004 a flash flood swept down Furnace Creek Wash and Highway 190. It swept away nine cars, and killed two people trapped in one car. Fifteen people were helicoptered to safety. The flood uprooted the toilets at Zabriskie Point, which

weighed 22 tons (20 metric tons) each, and carried them 100 feet (30 m). It tore up 13 miles (21 km) of highway, closing the park for nine days. It took nine months to repair Highway 190. The newspapers called it "a 100-year flood." How much rain caused all this damage?

   A) 1/3 of an inch (0.8 cm)   B) One inch (2.5 cm)
   C) Two inches (5 cm)

A. A) 1/3 of an inch (0.8 cm). In truth, it was probably more

---

In 1908 a mining engineer decided that Death Valley was, literally, the gateway to Hell.

like a 20-year flood. But the rains fell in areas that all funneled into Furnace Creek Wash, where it did more damage that it would have elsewhere.

Q. The flood of 2004 filled the Badwater salt pan with water. How deep was it?

  A) 6 inches (0.15 m)   B) 2 feet (0.6 m)   C) 3 feet (0.9 m)

A. C) 3 feet (0.9 m). People went kayaking at Badwater. The water dissolved all the salt formations, and when the water dried up, the salt flat really was flat.

In 1940 there was another flood down Furnace Creek Wash. Such floods had been normal for thousands of years, but now humans had built a highway down the wash, and a luxury hotel right beside it. The 1940 flood wiped out seven miles of highway. It also lifted up two borax wagons on display in front of Furnace Creek Inn and swept them away on what Borax Company manager Harry Gower called "the fastest run ever recorded" for borax wagons. The next year, construction crews diverted the channel of Furnace Creek Wash into Gower Gulch, a canyon that starts just south of Zabriskie Point and drains into the bottom of Death Valley. Until then, Gower Gulch had been a modest, narrow canyon that drained a local area. But now Gower Gulch was receiving the flood waters of a huge area. In the years since 1941, floods have turned Gower Gulch into a deep, wide canyon, packed with flood debris. The tail end of Gower Gulch is now threatening to cut into Furnace Creek Wash and cut Highway 190.

After a brief attempt in 1891, official weather observations in Death Valley started in 1911.

GEOLOGY
DEATH VALLEY ROCKS!

Q. Very few of the old-time prospectors had been to college, yet they had to be good geologists to recognize the types of rocks where gold or other precious metals might be found. But it took professional geologists to see the big picture of how geological forces had shaped Death Valley. The first geologist to devote a career to exploring Death Valley was Yale-educated Levi Noble. In the same way that old-time prospectors became devoted to their burros, Levi Noble did all his exploring of Death Valley in a vehicle that, by the time he retired in the 1950s, was considered an antique. What was it?

  A) A 1931 Model A Ford   B) A 1936 Ford truck   C) A 1940 Jeep

A. A) A 1931 Model A Ford car. Noble said that a Model A Ford was perfect for Death Valley because it had high clearance, good gears, and was mechanically simple. Noble's Model A Ford became legendary, and it went on display in the lobby of the national headquarters of the U.S. Geological Survey, next to an Apollo lunar rover.

> Levi Noble started his geological career mapping the Grand Canyon, where the rocks are arranged like a layer cake. But Death Valley geology is very different, as Noble explained: "The scenery of the Grand Cañon...is the expression of a rock structure whose order and simplicity are unequaled elsewhere. The scenery of the Death Valley region is the expression of a rock structure so chaotically disorganized that even its general nature was but recently recognized."

Q. True or false: As geologists define the word "valley," Death Valley isn't really a valley.
A. True. A valley is carved by water. Death Valley was created by tectonic forces. Death Valley is actually a "graben," where a section of Earth's crust has dropped down. Death Valley is also defined as a basin, the deepest basin in the Basin and Range province of the American West.

Q. What created the Basin and Range province?
A. It was created when two tectonic plates began to pull apart. In the myths of some Native Americans, Earth's surface is the shell of a giant turtle, and earthquakes are caused when the turtle moves. It turns out that this idea contains some geological truth. Earth's crust is made up of many large shells, 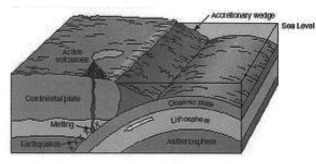 or tectonic plates, that are slowly pushed around by the currents of magma rising from deep inside the earth. In some places these plates collide and form mountain ranges, and in other places

Death Valley holds one of the longest fault lines in California.

these plates pull apart. About 15 million years ago, two tectonic plates began pulling apart. The boundary between them is the San Andreas Fault. The movement of these two plates causes earthquakes in California. As the plates have pulled apart, a large section of the American West has been stretched out by about 150 miles (241 km).

Q. How fast was the land separating?
   A) 0.001 inch (0.025 millimeter) per year
   B) 1 inch (2.5 cm) per year   C) 6 inches (15 cm) per year
A. B) About one inch (2.5 cm) per year. As the land has stretched out, Earth's crust has broken apart, and large blocks of it have slumped and tilted. These tilted sections are the mountain ranges of the Basin and Range province. The mountain ranges on both sides of Death Valley hold rock strata that are tilted at steep angles; this tilt can be hard to see from the valley floor, but it's obvious from places inside the mountains, such as Zabriskie Point and Aguereberry Point. To visualize the formation of the Basin and Range, imagine an accordion. As an accordion is stretched out, lots of ridges appear, and in between each ridge is a crease. The deepest of these creases is Death Valley.

Q. Why is Death Valley deeper than other basins in the Basin and Range province?
A. The answer is connected with why Mt. Whitney is taller than any other mountain in the Basin and Range. As the Basin and Range stretches, blocks of Earth's crust are tilting just like seesaws. As one end of a seesaw tilts up, the other end tilts down. If one end goes up unusually high, the other end has to go down unusually low. Death Valley is the low end of the same seesaw that lifted up the Panamint Mountains to the west. Mt. Whitney and the Sierras is the high end of another seesaw farther west.

Q. Why does this geological seesaw action create taller mountains and deeper valleys in Southern California than elsewhere?
A. The Basin and Range province has formed from east to west, and its western edge, which includes Death Valley, is still geologically active. Millions of years ago, when the Basin and Range was forming in Nevada, Nevada probably included valleys as deep as

---

Stovepipe Well spring permanently stopped flowing after an earthquake.

Death Valley and mountains as tall as Mt. Whitney. But erosion soon started wearing down those mountains and filling in those valleys. In southern California the mountain ranges and basins are still fairly new, so erosion hasn't had so much time to erase them. Death Valley has formed in the last three million years.

Q. Still, erosion has been at work in Death Valley. The valley floor holds lots of sediments washed down from the mountains on either side. How deep is this sediment?
  A) 200 feet (61 m)   B) 1,000 feet (305 m)
  C) 10,000 feet (3 km)
A. C) Under the floor of Death Valley, there's nearly 10,000 feet, or about 2 miles (3 km) of sediment. If this sediment wasn't there, Death Valley would be 2 miles (3 km) below sea level. Erosion has been doing its best to fill in Death Valley, but the valley has continued dropping faster than erosion can fill it up.

Q. About 2,000 years ago a big earthquake, estimated at 8 on the Richter scale, lowered the floor of Death Valley. How many feet did the valley drop?
  A) 2 feet (0.6 m)   B) 10 feet (3 m)   C) 20 feet (6 m)
A. C) 20 feet (6 m). You can still see evidence of this earthquake in the form of ridgelines on the alluvial fan just south of Badwater. The largest earthquake scientifically recorded in Death Valley was a magnitude 6.3 earthquake in 1993. It was centered in the Eureka Valley at the north end of the park, but it was strong enough to make cars wobble at Scotty's Castle.

Q. The mountains on either side of Death Valley are separated by a major fault line. The Panamint Range is sliding north, while the Amargosa Range is sliding south. By how many miles have these two mountain ranges already slid past one another?
  A) 2 miles (3.2 km)   B) 5 miles (8 km)   C) 30 miles (48 km)
A. C) 30 miles (48 km).

Q. In the southern end of Death Valley is a volcano, Cinder Hill, that's been ripped in half, with one half now sitting hundreds of feet away from the other half. How did this happen?
A. The volcano was sitting right atop a fault line. As the two sides

---

500 million years ago, as the continents drifted...

Death Valley Geology Made Simple

Geology in Death Valley can get so confusing that pioneer geologist Levi Noble called one whole region "the Amargosa Chaos." To make things less chaotic, here's how the big story shows up at some of Death Valley's most popular locations:

Badwater: The dark cliffs just north of Badwater are the oldest rocks in Death Valley, up to 1.8 billion years old. These are the same rocks that make up the bottom layer and the oldest rocks in the Grand Canyon.

Mosaic Canyon and Titus Canyon: For hundreds of millions of years, limestone was deposited at the bottom of the sea, limestone that would someday erode into twisting canyons.

Dantes View and the Panamint Mountains: About 15 million years ago, the Basin and Range province began forming, tilting blocks of the earth's crust into mountain ranges separated by basins.

Zabriskie Point, Artists Drive, Golden Canyon: As basins formed between ranges, many basins filled with lakes, and then the lakes filled with mud and clay, which would someday erode into colorful badlands.

Badwater, Devils Golf Course, Salt Creek, Harmony Borax Works: As Death Valley dried out after the last Ice Age, old lakebeds became large deposits of salt and borax.

Mesquite Flat Sand Dunes: Drying and erosion combined to create a desert, including sand dunes. The Mesquite Flat Sand Dunes formed about 10,000 years ago.

Scotty's Castle, Rhyolite: There'd been gold in them thar' hills for 100 million years. At long last, someone got excited about it.

...the future location of Death Valley was at the equator.

Titus Canyon

of the fault continued sliding past one another, each carried half of the volcano with it.

Q. When you hike up many Death Valley canyons you soon come to tall, impassible ledges, but in Titus Canyon the gradient is so gradual that you can drive through it. What's the difference?

A. The Black Mountains (which includes popular hikes like Natural Bridge and Artists Palette), are on an active fault line, which is lifting up the mountains faster than erosion can cut through the rock. This leaves ledges. But Titus Canyon is in the Grapevine Mountains, which isn't being uplifted so fast, so erosion has had a chance to even out the drainage.

Q. For most geologists the most impressive thing about Death Valley is:

    A) Its mountains   B) Its valley floor

    C) Its alluvial fans (those large slopes of rock debris)

A. C) Its alluvial fans. The phrase "alluvial fan" comes from the word "alluvium," which is rock, dirt, sand, and gravel that have been carried and deposited by flowing water. When it rains hard in Death Valley, water rushes through canyons, carrying many tons of rock debris. When floodwaters exit canyons and spread out into the wide-open valley, they lose force and begin dropping their debris, forming fan-shaped slopes. The alluvial fans in Death Valley are some of the largest in the world, and since there is little vegetation to cover them, the fans are easy to see. As you drive up these alluvial fans on your way to Artists Palette, Natural Bridge, or Titus Canyon, you too can join "the alluvial fan club."

Q. The alluvial fans on the west side (Panamint Mountain side) of Death Valley are much larger than on the east side (Dantes

---

Golden Canyon rocks hold the ripple marks of ancient lakes.

View side). On the west side the fans are usually 1,000 feet (305 m) thick and extend three to five miles (5-8 km) in length. The largest fans are as thick as 6,000 feet (1,828 m). On the east side the largest fan is only 400 feet (122 m) thick and one mile (1.6 km) long. Why are west-side fans so much larger?

A) The Panamint Mountains are twice as high as east-side mountains.

B) The Panamints get more rain.

C) The floor of Death Valley actually slopes downward toward the east, which means that rock debris flowing off the Panamints is going downhill, while debris from east-side mountains is—as soon as it hits the valley floor—flowing uphill.

D) All of the above

A. D) All of the above.

Q. Geologically speaking, the kids playing on the Mesquite Flat Sand Dunes have something in common with Death Valley gold prospectors. What?

A. Both played with quartz. Gold was found in veins of quartz, a whitish rock embedded in granite. Sand is mostly tiny pieces of quartz. Quartz eroded out of quartz veins high up in the mountains and broke into smaller and smaller pieces as it worked its way to the valley floor, where it piled up as sand dunes. Considering how few prospectors found gold, the kids playing on the dunes are probably having more fun with quartz than the prospectors ever did.

Q. What percent of Death Valley National Park is made of sand dunes?

A) One percent   B) 5 percent   C) 10 percent

A. A) One percent.

Q. Some sand dunes look like waves—with row upon row of regular crests. Others look like stars, with several ridges curving down from a peak. What causes sand dunes to have different shapes?

A) The size of sand grains   B) Winds   C) Rain and erosion

A. B) Winds. Winds are what create sand dunes to begin with. The wind blows sand into pockets in the landscape where the sand can't get out, so the sand continues piling up. In the case of the Mesquite Flat Sand Dunes, it's not a trap in the landscape but

---

Death Valley gift shops sell borax jewelry called "Death Valley Pearls."

a pattern of converging winds that keeps the sand "corralled." Where winds blow steadily from one direction, they build wave-like dunes. If the wind shifts in several directions, it builds stars or other shapes, like at Mesquite Flat.

Q. How fast do winds need to blow before they can move sand grains?
A) 10 miles (16 km) per hour   B) 20 miles (32 km) per hour
C) 30 miles (48 km) per hour

A. A) 10 miles (16 km) per hour—just a breeze. At this speed, sand grains begin to roll or bounce along the ground. With more wind, sand starts flying. In strong winds, dark clouds of sand swirl into the air. In pioneer days, sandstorms at Mesquite Flat covered up the original Stovepipe Well spring, which is why people stuck a stovepipe in it to mark its location. Today, people hiking at Mesquite Flat during a sandstorm may have trouble finding their cars, and may find their windshields pitted. Wind turns tents into kites, and once blew down the front wall of the Stovepipe Wells ranger station.

Ibex Dunes

Q. True or false: Sand dunes are like sponges, holding lots more water than the rocky desert.
A. True. If you dig a hole deep enough into a sand dune, you'll find moist sand, even in the summer. This means that sand dunes can support lots of plants. The Eureka Dunes have 50 plant species, including two endangered species.

Q. How tall are Death Valley's sand dunes?
A) 140 feet (42 m)   B) 400 feet (121 m)
C) 700 feet (213 m)
A. C) The tallest dunes in the park, the Eureka Dunes, are up to 700 feet (213 m) tall. This is tall enough to bury the St. Louis

Death Valley holds a thin layer of ash from volcanic eruptions in Yellowstone...

Gateway Arch, and it would come halfway to the top of the Willis Tower (formerly the Sears), the tallest building in America at 1,451 feet (442 m). The Mesquite Flat Sand Dunes are about 140 feet (42 m) tall.

Q. True or false: Sand dunes can make a thundering sound.
A. True. If a dune is steep enough and dry enough, its sliding sands—set loose by human footsteps—make a strange, deep noise, like thunder. (The Mesquite Flat Sand Dunes aren't steep enough to thunder).

> "The dunes suggested Egyptian architecture; the pyramids and the crouching sphinx were there...What is the huge sphinx, brooding and massive, gazing with strong eyes across the emptiness, but an interpretation of the desert carved in stone?"
> —Edna Brush Perkins, *The White Heart of Mojave*

Q. Death Valley has lots of sand and lots of wind and lots of rocks for the blowing sand to hit. What happens to those rocks?
A. They are sand-blasted into odd shapes. Water causes most of the erosion in Southwestern deserts, but Death Valley is one place where wind erosion is visible. Geologists call sand-blasted rocks "ventifacts" from "ventus," the Latin word for wind. Caltech geologist Robert P. Sharp was so impressed by the sand-blasted rocks on one ridge (across the highway from the entrance to Artists Drive) that he called it "Ventifact Ridge."

Q. In the salt pan, how far down does the salt go?
  A) 25 feet (7.6 m)   B) 100 feet (30 m)   C) 1,000 feet (305 m)
A. C) Drill holes in the salt pan showed that it goes down about 1,000 feet (305 m). Layers of salt alternate with layers of clay and dirt. The clay and dirt accumulated in periods of wetter climate, when rains washed lots of sediment down from the mountains, and even formed lakes on the valley floor. During drier periods, the lakes disappeared, leaving a layer of salt. The top layer of salt, which you walk on at Badwater, is from one to six feet (0.3 to 1.8 m) thick, with mud underneath.

...600 miles (965 km) away, 640,000 years ago.

Q. Why does the salt pan at Badwater form polygonal slabs?
A. Underneath the salt is a layer of mud, which dries out and cracks apart, forming polygons. Mud behaves like this everywhere. When you add a thick layer of salt that is crystallizing in the sun, it looks even stranger. The salt pan looks different in different places because of different mixtures of mud, sand, salt, and water.

Death Valley salt flat

Q. The salt formations at Devils Golf Course are much taller than at Badwater. Why is this?
A. Devils Golf Course is higher in elevation, so it doesn't get the occasional floodwaters that dissolve the salt formations at Badwater.

Q. What forms the salt pinnacles at Badwater and Devils Golf Course?
A. Just below the surface there's lots of water, which evaporates and leaves deposits of salt. As the salt builds up, the water continues rising through it, as if the sun is drinking through a straw made of salt. The salt formations continue growing higher, but rain and wind are always eroding them.

Q. If you listen carefully at Devils Golf Course, you may hear the sound of "snap, crackle, pop." What is it?
A. As the salt formations heat up, moisture is sucked out of them, and billions of salt crystals expand and pop. Elsewhere, salt penetrates into cracks in rocks, and as heat causes the salt to expand, it can break up rocks, just like water does when it freezes.

Q. Like many miners, Harry Gower, a Borax Company executive who helped start tourism in Death Valley, had a fondness for dynamite. In the 1920s he set off dynamite blasts in the Devils Golf Course as entertainment for tourists, and to reveal the water just below the surface. Is there any trace left of these explosions?

Just as the glare from snow can cause "snow blindness"...

A. No, the quick-growing salt formations long ago healed the scars of the dynamite blasts.

Q. The purity of the salt in the Death Valley salt pan varies from place to place. How close does the salt at Badwater come to being pure table salt?
   A) 30 percent   B) 75 percent   C) 95 percent
A. C) 95 percent. Taste it for yourself. It was such good salt that during World War Two, a football-field-sized area of the Badwater salt pan was mined for salt.

Q. In a remote, hard-to-reach area of Death Valley, there's a *playa* (a very flat, usually dry lakebed) where rocks move mysteriously. How big is the largest of the rocks that's been known to move?
   A) One pound (0.45 kg)   B) 27 pounds (12 kg)
   C) 1,275 pounds (578 kg)
A. C) 1, 275 pounds (578 kg). All of the rocks have female names, a tradition started by Caltech geologist Robert P. Sharp, who studied the moving rocks in the 1960s. The 1,275-pound rock is named Kitty. The smallest moving rock, Hanna, weighs 0.96 pounds (435 grams).

Q. The rocks leave shallow tracks on the playa, so we know how far they've moved. How long is the longest track?
 A) 25 feet (7.6 m)   B) 254 feet (77 m)   C) 2,439 feet (743 m)
A. C) 2,439 feet (743 m), or nearly half a mile, traveled by Diane.

Q. The playa with the moving rocks is called the Racetrack. True or false: The Racetrack was named for the moving rocks.
A. False. The name "Racetrack" first appeared on a map in 1913. The moving rocks weren't noticed until 1915, by prospector Joseph Crook. The Racetrack was named for its circular shape and a rocky ridge called "The Grandstand." Crook's wife conducted the first study of the moving rocks by marking their position to see if they really were moving.

Q. Do all of the Racetrack rocks move in the same direction?
A. In general, yes. But there are lots of zigzags and curves along the way.

...visitors to Badwater sometimes suffer from "salt blindness."

Q. Are the rocks moving downhill?
A. No, the Racetrack is pretty flat. In fact, the north end, to-ward which the rocks are moving, is a few centimeters higher than the south end, so to a tiny degree the rocks are actually moving *uphill*.

Q. What causes the rocks to move?
   A) Earthquakes
   B) Flash floods
   C) Wind
   D) Pranksters
   E) Magnetic forces from UFOs flying out of Area 51
A. C) Wind! The mountainous landscape around the Racetrack acts like a giant wind tunnel, causing winds of up to 100 miles (160 km) per hour. The Racetrack surface is very smooth, and when it is lubricated by a bit of rain, the rocks can glide along like little sailboats.

Q. In 1953 geologist John Shelton landed his small airplane on the Racetrack and used its propeller to test the theory that wind could move the rocks. He also brought some water to wet the playa surface. His propeller generated only a 42 mile (67 km) per hour wind. Was this enough to move a rock?
A. Yes, but only a small, 19-ounce (532 grams) rock, and not far.

Q. In the 1990s geologist Paula Messina studied 162 rocks whose tracks showed they'd moved. Which rocks traveled farther, the larger ones or the smaller ones?
A. The tracks of the smaller rocks averaged 833 feet (254 m), while the tracks of the larger rocks averaged 348 feet (106 m). But the size of the rocks was less important than their location on the playa—some parts of the playa get a lot more wind than others. Rounder rocks produced the most curving tracks, while more jagged rocks traveled straighter, perhaps because they had a "rudder."

Q. Death Valley is more famous for prospecting and mining than most of the American West. Is this because Death Valley had more minerals than other areas?

The road to the Racetrack is so bad, even park rangers
have gotten stranded...

A. Not really. Similar-sized areas nearby probably had just as many minerals and mines, and only a few Death Valley mines were really productive. Death Valley's fame comes from the 20-mule team used in national advertising for decades, and from the mystique of prospectors who braved the toughest desert in America.

Q. Where are precious metals found in Death Valley?
   A) In the valley   B) In the mountains
A. B) In the mountains. Gold and silver occur in veins inside solid rock, such as granite. There isn't much solid rock on the valley floor. But this is where you find borax, which has washed down from the mountains above.

Q. Borax is a form of boron, one of the chemical elements. Boron is a rare element to begin with, and it accumulates only in rare circumstances, where it washes out of mountains and settles onto dry lake beds. Borax is found in only five deserts on Earth. What is the earliest-known human use of borax?
   A) The ancient Egyptians used it to preserve mummies.
   B) By 800 AD, Arab goldsmiths used it to process gold.
   C) Benjamin Franklin discovered its use as soap.
A. B) While legend says that the Egyptians used it for preserving mummies, there's no proof of this. Arab goldsmiths are the first known users of borax. The word "borax" comes from the Arab word for "white."

Q. Why are the bad-lands around Zabriskie Point totally bare of plants?
A. The ground is made of clay, which doesn't absorb much water. These clays also erode into exotic, colorful shapes.

From Zabriskie Point

...Geologist Paula Messina shredded 13 tires there over the years.

Q. What forms the odd colors at Artists Palette?
A. About 6 to 8 million years ago volcanoes in the area pumped out a lot of ash, which settled onto a clay-rich lake and produced some unusual chemical reactions. Geologists are still puzzling over the details.

Q. Rocks in deserts are often coated dark by "desert varnish." What is this?
A. The desert wind is full of clay and brushes it onto rock surfaces. The sun bakes the clay onto the rock. Bacteria metabolize the clay into manganese, which is black. The darkness of desert varnish can tell you how long rocks have been exposed to the air. If a cliff caves off, the newly-exposed layer may be much lighter than the rock around it. In Death Valley alluvial fans, the darker rocks are the older flows. Native Americans create petroglyphs by scratching off desert varnish.

> "It seemed strange that such barrenness could exhibit this radiance of color, but nothing could have been more beautiful."
>
> —Frank Norris, *McTeague*

Q. At the northern tip of the Cottonwood Mountains, there's a deep hole called Ubehebe Crater (pronounced *YOU-bee-HEE-bee*), which is named for a Native American word meaning "big basket in the rock." The crater is half a mile (1 km) wide. How deep is it?
  A) Equal to the drop of Niagara Falls
  B) Equal to the height of the Statue of Liberty
  C) Equal to the height of the Washington Monument
A. C) The Washington Monument is 555 feet tall, and Ubehebe Crater ranges from 500 feet to 777 feet deep (150 to 237 m)

Q. Ubehebe Crater was formed by:
  A) A meteorite
  B) A volcanic eruption
  C) An underground steam explosion
A. C) An underground steam explosion. Since most craters on Earth are extinct volcanoes, it's often tricky for geologists to recognize the exceptions, especially when there's some volcanic

---

For the Timbisha Shoshone, Ubehebe Crater was where...

debris in and around the crater, as there is at Ubehebe Crater. But Ubehebe Crater was formed when underground magma came into contact with underground water. The water turned into steam and built up pressure until there was a big explosion that tossed 600 feet (182 m) of rock in all directions.

Q. When did Ubehebe Crater blow up?
A. This has been a tough question for geologists to pin down. Until recently they said 3,000 to 6,000 years ago. The latest research, which used radiocarbon dating techniques on vegetation that was buried by the explosion, says only 300 years ago. An indirect confirmation of this date comes from the oral traditions of the Timbisha Shoshone, who are still passing down stories about the explosion.

Q. Devils Hole, a deep, narrow, water-filled cave, acts like a giant eardrum to "hear" earthquakes from around the world. In reaction to the 2002 Alaska earthquake (7.9 on the Richter scale), the water in Devils Hole bobbed up and down. How much did it go up and down?
   A) One inch (2.5 cm)   B) One foot (0.3 m)
   C) 6 feet (1.8 m)
A. C) 6 feet. And for a 6.6 earthquake in Pakistan, on the opposite side of the world, the water in Devils Hole bobbed by a few inches.

Q. Are there any dinosaur bones or footprints in Death Valley?
A. No, during the age of the dinosaurs most of the Death Valley area was under the sea. But Titanothere Canyon was named for the fossil of a 40-million-year-old rhinoceros-like mammal found there. Old mudstones in Death Valley contain the footprints of mastodons, camels, big cats, and birds.

...humans first emerged into the world.

WILD LIFE

EVEN THE PLANTS

ARE WILD AND CRAZY

Q. Which group of animals has more species in Death Valley: reptiles or mammals?

A. You might think that Death Valley should be a paradise for reptiles, but there are 38 species of reptiles and 56 species of mammals. Of reptiles, there are 18 lizards, 19 snakes, and the desert tortoise. Yet some people might consider these reptiles to be less creepy than many of the mammals. A third of Death Valley's mammals are bats, and half are rodents. Death Valley is a tough place for larger mammals, but they include desert bighorn sheep, mountain lions, bobcats, and coyotes.

Q. One Death Valley creature is the road runner, made famous by the cartoon. In fact, Death Valley is more typical of road-runner habitat than is the scenery in the cartoon, whose spires and arches are more typical of the high-altitude, red-rock deserts of Utah. Road runners are found in lower-altitude, hotter deserts like the Mojave. True or false: road runners are birds.
A. True, but they seldom fly. They might lift themselves a few feet off the ground, for maybe 30 yards (27 m). They prefer to run. Their feet are specially adapted for running, leaving an X-shaped footprint, in contrast with the Y-shaped footprints of most birds.

Q. Do the coyotes in Death Valley chase road runners, as in the cartoon?
A. Young coyotes may try to catch road runners, but they soon learn their lesson. Road runners can really run! Adult coyotes don't even try. No biologist has ever witnessed a coyote catching a road runner. In that respect, the cartoon is good science. But road runners don't go "beep, beep," and no biologist has ever seen a coyote run straight off a cliff, or get bonked by his own anvil.

Q. Which animal can accelerate faster?

    A) An Olympic sprinter
    B) A champion race horse
    C) A road runner
A. C) A road runner. However, the road runner can't keep up the pace. A road runner can run at 20 miles (32 km) per hour, while a human can sprint at 24 miles (38 km) per hour, and a horse can run at 38 miles (61 km) per hour.

Q. What does a road runner eat?
    A) Rattlesnakes   B) Scorpions   C) Poisonous spiders
    D) All of the above
A. D) All of the above. Road runners will eat just about anything, including lizards, insects, rodents, seeds, and fruit.

Q. How does a road runner catch a rattlesnake?
A. Very carefully. A road runner jumps and flutters around a

Coyotes range up to 100 miles (161 km) to hunt.

rattlesnake, goading it to strike, and then the road runner grabs the snake by the head and pounds the head against a rock. Road runners contain anti-venom that helps protect them from rattlesnake bites.

Q. For humans, normal body temperature is 98.6 F (37 C). What is the normal temperature of a road runner?
   A) 90 F (32 C)   B) 104 F (40 C)   C) 120 F (49 C)
A. B) 104 F (40C). This high metabolism gives road runners a higher tolerance for heat. Road runners are active during the day.

Q. Coyotes in Death Valley are smaller than elsewhere, reflecting the scarcity of food. How much do they weigh?
   A) 20 pounds (9 kg)   B) 30 pounds (14 kg)
   C) 50 pounds (23 kg)
A. B) Around 30 pounds (14 kg). They are about two feet (0.6 m) high at the shoulder. From the nose to the tip of the tail they might be five feet (1.5 m) long.

Q. What do coyotes eat?
A. Coyotes try to catch rodents, birds, or lizards, but they'll settle for a meal of mesquite beans. They'll also kill pet dogs that are allowed to run loose or are left outside an RV at night. Coyotes have grabbed beefsteaks right off of campground picnic tables.

Q. True or false: Death Valley coyotes enjoy playing golf.
A. True. At the golf course at Furnace Creek Ranch, young coyotes sometimes chase golf balls. They'll even grab the golf balls in their mouths, run up a hill, let the golf ball loose, chase it down the slope, grab it again, and run back up the hill, repeating this game over and over.

Chipmunks can range over 15 acres (6 ha).

Q. Death Valley has jackrabbits—those rabbits with the big feet and big ears. Why are their ears so large?
  A) For hearing coyotes sneaking up   B) For air conditioning
  C) To disguise them as cactus
A. B) For air conditioning. The ears are lined with millions of tiny blood vessels, which bring blood close to the surface so that body heat can radiate away. Including its ears, a jackrabbit is 28 inches (71 cm) tall, or over two feet.

Q. With its large feet, a jackrabbit can run fast. How fast?
  A) 15 miles (24 km) per hour   B) 25 miles (40 km) per hour
  C) 35 miles (56 km) per hour
A. C) 35 miles (56 km) per hour, at least for a short burst—but long enough to discourage a coyote. Jackrabbits can make long leaps, spin in the air, and come down running in another direction.

Q. The largest mammal in Death Valley is the desert bighorn sheep. How much do they weigh?
  A) 150 pounds (68 kg)   B) 300 pounds (136 kg)
  C) 400 pounds (181 kg)
A. A) Around 150 pounds (68 kg), for a mature ram. Elsewhere in the Southwest, desert bighorn sheep can get up to 300 pounds (136 kg), but as with other animals, Death Valley bighorns are smaller. Their weight fluctuates with the seasons. After a spring of good eating, a ram may get up to 200 pounds (90 kg), but by winter it may have lost 1/3 of this weight.

Q. Desert bighorn sheep are well adapted for desert survival. They can even allow their body temperature to rise temporarily to 107 F (42 C), which would kill many other animals. They can go without water for three days in summer, ten days in winter. When they do drink, how much of their body weight can they drink?
  A) 10 percent   B) 20 percent   C) 30 percent
A. C) 30 percent. But in summer they usually stay near water sources so they can drink daily. Bighorns can get by on 2/3 of a gallon (2.5 L) per day.

Q. How many desert bighorn sheep are found in Death Valley?
A. Desert bighorn sheep live in remote areas, so it's a bit tricky

---

Kangaroo rats can leap 10 feet (3 m) in one jump.

to be sure of their numbers. It's probably around 600. But it used to be much higher. Biologists estimate that Death Valley once supported as many as 4,800 bighorn sheep, and could again.

Q. Why did the desert bighorn sheep population decline so much?

    A) Hunting by humans   B) Competition from burros
    C) The climate dried out.

A. B) Competition from burros. "Burro" is the Spanish word for donkey, a word usually used for the smaller donkeys that prospectors used as pack animals. Prospectors preferred burros over horses or mules because burros needed less water and food but were big enough to carry a prospector's gear. Prospectors introduced burros into Death Valley, but many burros escaped or were turned loose, and they began breeding a wild population. When Death Valley

became a national monument in 1933, the wild burro population had risen to 2,000, and the desert bighorn sheep population was down to 300 and falling. Burros may be lovable characters and part of Wild West history, but they also pose big problems for native wildlife, especially desert bighorn sheep. Burros are natives of Africa and don't fit the ecosystems of American deserts. They eat about 6,000 pounds (2,721 kg) of forage per year—three times as much as bighorns. Instead of eating only the leaves, burros rip up entire plants. Burros drink more than twice as much water as bighorns, and they aggressively guard springs, keeping away other animals, including bighorns. In spite of their horns, desert bighorn sheep are actually shy animals. In the 1980s wildlife biologists removed 5,643 burros from the Death Valley region. The bighorn population has been recovering very slowly.

Q. Are there deer in Death Valley?

A. Not on the valley floor; there isn't enough vegetation. There are deer high up in the Panamint Mountains, where there are trees. Even during a wildflower bloom that turns the valley green, deer won't come down from the mountains.

Burros are so tough, they'll fight off mountain lions.

Q. Kangaroo rats have a unique ability that helps them survive in the desert. What is it?
  A) They don't need to drink water.
  B) They tolerate high heat.
  C) They eat sand.
A. A) They don't need to drink water. They can metabolize water out of the foods they eat. And they have other adaptations that help them conserve water: they have no sweat glands; their nasal passages recover water vapor as they exhale; and their urine and feces are highly concentrated.

Q. Pioneers in Death Valley and the rest of the Southwest sometimes woke up to find that something of theirs had disappeared during the night. They weren't surprised if food had disappeared, but sometimes the missing object was a coin, eyeglasses, or a spoon. These disappearing objects probably led to some angry accusations of theft. But some people noticed that in the very spot where the missing object had been, a new object had appeared—a twig, a bone, a berry. What was going on?
A. The missing objects were being taken by pack rats, which got the nickname "trade rats" because they often left something in place of what they took. Some people decided that the pack rat was a noble animal who was trying to make a fair trade. More likely, the rats were carrying something back to their nest when they came upon something they liked more—shiny things do seem to appeal to them. They couldn't carry more than one thing, so they dropped a berry to take a coin.

Q. Pack rats build huge nests under rock ledges, using plant materials, including thorns to keep predators away. The rats cement the nests together with their urine, which helps the nests last a long time. Biologists have used carbon-14 dating techniques to date pack-rat nests in Death Valley. How old was one nest?
  A) 200 years   B) 900 years   C) 19,000 years

Death Valley's few mountain lions...

A. C) 19,000 years. This nest was built in the Ice Age, and included plants that no longer grow in Death Valley.

Q. The first bat seen fluttering in a Death Valley evening is often the western pipistrelle, the smallest bat in the United States. How much does it weigh?
  A) ¼ ounce (7 grams)   B) ¼ pound (113 grams)
  C) One pound (454 grams)
A. A) ¼ ounce (7 grams). It's about 3 inches (7.6 cm) long.

Q. True or false: Death Valley is too dry for amphibians.
A. False. There are five species of frogs and toads in Death Valley springs, though two were introduced by humans.

Q. The desert tortoise has survived in the toughest Southwestern deserts for millions of years. True or false: The floor of Death Valley is too hot and dry for the desert tortoise.
A. True. But you will find small numbers of desert tortoises above 3,000 feet (914 m) in elevation, where there's more vegetation. Tortoises can't travel far to find food, so they need a sufficient concentration of it. They gorge on spring wildflowers, and then they can go for months without eating, staying in burrows to avoid the summer heat.

Q. What's the difference between a tortoise and a turtle?
A. Tortoises live on land, while almost all turtles live in water. For digging, tortoises have much heavier legs than turtles, and strong claws. Desert tortoises have dug burrows as long as 32 feet (9.7 m), and as deep as 12 feet (3.6 m).

Q. How long can a desert tortoise go without drinking water?
  A) One week   B) One month   C) One year
A. C) One year. Desert tortoises absorb lots of moisture from the plants they eat.

...are high in the Panamint Mountains.

Q. As a species, how old are desert tortoises?
   A) 1 million years   B) 25 million years
   C) 200 million years
A. C) 200 million years. Desert tortoises are the oldest reptile species still living. As individuals, the oldest-known tortoise was 50 years old, and they may live twice that long. But desert tortoises take about 15 years to reach maturity, and 98 percent die before that age. Because of human impacts, the desert tortoise is now an endangered species.

Q. The most common rattlesnake in Death Valley is called the sidewinder. How did it get this name?
A. The sidewinder moves by whipping its body sideways. This motion leaves odd, J-shaped tracks on sand dunes. It also has the advantage of minimizing a snake's contact with very hot sand. The sidewinder is smaller than most rattlesnakes, about two feet (0.6 m) long, and its venom isn't as strong. Sidewinders are sometimes called "horned rattlesnakes" because of the raised scales over their eyes.

Q. The Mojave Desert rattlesnake is the most poisonous rattlesnake in America, with venom several times what it takes to kill a human. It is about four feet (1.2 m) long, and has a triangular head. To be safe, how far away should you stay from a Mojave Desert rattler?
   A) 2.5 feet (0.8 m)   B) 10 feet (3 m)   C) 100 feet (30 m)
A. A) 2.5 feet (0.8 m)—at least! A rattlesnake can strike a target only half as far away as its own body length. But you'd better not stick around to test this theory!

Q. The king snake will kill two of the following three animals. Which two?
   A) Humans   B) Rattlesnakes   C) Its own young
A. B & C. King snakes aren't poisonous, so they can't harm humans. The king snake is immune to rattlesnake venom, and will kill a rattlesnake by coiling around it and choking it. King snakes will also cannibalize their own young.

Q. True or false: Death Valley has a snake that is blind and toothless.
A. True. Like many snakes, the western blind snake hunts by

---

*In the early 1900s, a ranch near Death Valley raised
rattlesnakes for meat.*

sensing vibrations and heat, and it doesn't need teeth for its diet of ants and termites.

Q. Scorpions are an ancient life form. How long ago did scorpions arise?
A) 150 million years ago (before birds)
B) 250 million years ago (before dinosaurs)
C) 400 million years ago (before amphibians)
A. C) 400 million years ago. They were one of the first animals on land.

Q. True or false: The tarantula, a large, hairy spider, is very dangerous to humans.
A. False. Tarantula venom was made to kill insects, not large animals. Tarantula bites are no worse than bee stings. But due to its large size, the tarantula has often been cast as a monster in Hollywood movies.

Q. Tarantulas sometimes make a purring sound. Why?
A) Someone is petting them.
B) They are snoring.
C) As a warning.
A. C) To warn predators, tarantulas rub their legs together to make a purring sound. They also rely on their legs to sense vibrations in the ground, which signal movements. Though tarantulas have eight eyes, they don't see well.

Q. Though Hollywood movies may exaggerate the dangers of tarantulas, one thing that happens to tarantulas is straight out of a horror movie. The tarantula hawk is a large wasp that stings and paralyzes tarantulas. What does the wasp do next?
A. The tarantula hawk lays its eggs in the flesh of the tarantula and buries the tarantula alive. The larvae of the wasp then grow inside the paralyzed spider, eating it alive from the inside.

---

*The largest Death Valley snake is the gopher snake,
7 feet (2.1 m) long.*

Q. Does Death Valley have Gila monsters?
A. No, Death Valley is too hot and dry even for Gila monsters.

Q. The desert horned lizard, often called the horny toad, feeds on ants, which are not very nourishing. To digest lots of ants, the desert horned lizard has the largest stomach of any lizard species. What portion of its body, by weight, consists of stomach?
  A) 5 percent   B) 10 percent   C) 13 percent
A. C) 13 percent. Another talent of the desert horned lizard is that to defend itself, it can squirt blood from its eyes, hitting a target up to 6 feet (1.8 m) away.

Q. The Mojave fringe-toed lizard, as the name implies, has a special shape to its toes, which enables it to run fast. The zebra-tailed lizard stands on its rear legs to run. In a race between a fringe-toed lizard and a zebra-tailed lizard, which would win?
A. The fringe-toed lizard can run 10 miles (16 km) per hour, but it's a slowpoke compared with the zebra-tailed lizard, which can run 18 miles (29 km) per hour. Both lizards will run even when they are not being chased, since desert sands are *hot*.

Q. Chuckwallas are chubby and slow lizards. To defend themselves, they crawl into rock crevices and inflate their stomachs, wedging themselves in. What did Native Americans do to get them out?
A. Native Americans got a sharp stick, punctured the stomach, and pulled the chuckwalla out. If chuckwallas avoided this fate, they could live 40 years.

Q. What does the gecko do for an "insurance policy"?
A. Geckos store so much fat in their tails that they can stay underground for nine months, living off this fat. If a gecko is being pursued, it can break off its tail, which the predator grabs while the gecko gets away.

Q. If you see anthills in Death Valley, they probably belong to har-

---

The Mojave Desert's giant desert scorpion is the largest scorpion n the U.S., growing up to 3 inches.

vester ants. Their tunnels can go down 25 feet (7.6 m). Harvester ants got their name because they gather seeds. One ant colony can gather two million seeds in one year. An individual harvester ant can carry many times its own weight. How many times?

   A) 10   B) 20   C) 50

A. C) 50 times its own weight. Since the flowering season in Death Valley is so short, harvester ants need to reproduce quickly; unlike most ant colonies, which have only one queen to lay eggs, harvester ants may have 15 queen ants.

Q. How many species of birds have been counted in Death Valley?

   A) 100   B) 200   C) 400

A. C) Nearly 400—and counting. The first biological inventory of Death Valley, in 1891, counted 78 species. Dedicated bird watchers have continued spotting new species, though most of these birds  are just migrating through. Of year-round residents, the most noticeable is the raven, which is so smart and adaptable it can also live in the arctic. Birds of prey include red-tailed hawks, golden eagles, and peregrine falcons. Turkey vultures are common, except in winter. You may not see owls, but they see you. Smaller birds include wrens, sparrows, swallows, and swifts. The black-throated sparrow can derive water from its food, just like the kangaroo rat does. In migration season, you may see water birds like pelicans, ospreys, or herons. When the Harmony Borax Works was operating, ducks sometimes landed in the large vats used to crystallize borax, and if the ducks stayed all night, their feathers became so soaked in borax that the ducks were too heavy to take off.

Q. With so few trees in Death Valley, where do birds nest?

A. Even where there are trees, ravens and red-tailed hawks prefer to nest high up on cliffs, which offer shelter and a good view. Smaller birds—especially hummingbirds—may nest in bushes. Road runners and Gambel's quail nest on the ground.

Creosote bushes have survived nuclear test-blasts
that killed all other plants.

Q. True or false: There are fish in Death Valley.
A. True. The springs and pools in Death Valley support small fish, including nine species found nowhere else.

Q. How did fish get to Death Valley?
A. They swam. In the Ice Age, Death Valley held a large lake, Lake Manly, which was connected with other lakes in the region, and with the Colorado River. As the climate dried out, most of the fish in Death Valley died out, but a few species were able to withstand Death Valley's warm, salty water.

Q. Death Valley has five species of pupfish, which got its name because of its frisky, puppy-like behavior. Pupfish are small, no longer than 2.5 inches. Biologists believe that in the Ice Age there was

only one species of pupfish in Death Valley, but it became five different species. How did this happen?
A. As Lake Manly dried up, the pupfish were left stranded in widely isolated pools, which had different sizes, temperatures, salt contents, and food supplies. To survive in different conditions, the pupfish evolved in different ways, until they had become five species.

Q. The size of pupfish habitat varies greatly. The Salt Creek habitat is over one mile (1.6 km) long, at least in the cooler seasons. The Devils Hole pupfish lives in the thin top layer of an underwater cave. What is the total area of this cave opening?
    A) 23 square yards (19 sq m)   B) 230 sq yards (192 sq m)
    C) 523 sq yards (437 sq m)
A. A) 23 square yards (19 sq m). This is the smallest habitat of any invertebrate in the world. While the Devils Hole cave goes down a long way, only its top layer gets enough sunlight to grow the algae the pupfish eat. The water is 92 F (33 C). The population of pupfish fluctuates, and has gotten as low as 100. Today the pupfish is threatened by agricultural wells that are lowering the regional water table, including the water in Devils Hole. Death Valley National Park biologists have made heroic efforts to save the Devils Hole pupfish from extinction.

Death Valley has eight species of snails, all living in springs...

Q. Death Valley's pupfish live in water that is far too salty for humans to drink. Compared with seawater, how salty is it?

A) Equal to seawater   B) Twice as salty   C) Five times as salty

A. C) At Cottonball Marsh, the pupfish live in water five times as salty as the ocean. At Salt Creek, the salt content is equal to seawater.

Q. True or false: When Salt Creek dries up in summer, the pupfish survive by burrowing into the mud and hibernating.

A. False, but people once believed this. Only the pupfish that retreat to the springs at the head of the creek survive. Those stranded below become snacks for coyotes.

Q. How many species of plants are found in Death Valley?

A) 250   B) 750   C) 1,000

A. C) About 1,000 species have been identified, but with all the remote areas in Death Valley, there are undoubtedly many species still unknown. This surprisingly high number is because of Death Valley's variations in altitude, which create many variations of climate. This 1,000 plants includes 20 plants that are endemic—found no where else on Earth.

Q. For desert plants, which portion is bigger: the part underground, or the part above ground?

A. Because desert plants need extensive root systems to find water, the part underground is almost always larger than the part above ground. Mesquite roots may go down 60 feet (18m) or more, several times the height of mesquite branches.

Q. In one square yard of Mojave Desert soil, how many seeds are there?

A) 25   B) 2,500   C) 25,000

A. C) 25,000. Most of these seeds are so small you'd need a microscope to see them. These seeds come from up to 200 types of plants. Desert plants need to produce a lot of seeds to make sure a few of them find a good spot.

Q. The most common shrub in Death Valley is the creosote. Creosotes are noted for their strong scent, which is even stronger

---

...like the pupfish, they are relics of a vanished, wetter Ice Age.

after a rain. You can also stimulate this scent by cupping your hands around creosote leaves and blowing on them. Creosote bushes are evenly spaced, with large gaps between them. True or false: these gaps are there because creosote bushes use chemical warfare against other plants.

A. True. Creosote bushes secrete a chemical that kills other plants, even other creosotes, giving each creosote bush enough space to gain a sufficient water supply.

Q. Creosote bushes reproduce by cloning, by sending out underground shoots. This means that creosotes spread outward in a

ring-like pattern. One known creosote ring is 40 feet (12 m) across. How old is the oldest creosote bush?
A) 100 years   B) 750 years   C) 11,000 years
A. C) 11,000 years, if you define today's plant as the same plant that's been cloning itself all this time. Creosote bushes were the first plant to colonize the Mojave Desert at the end of the last Ice Age. Some of today's creosote rings were started by an original colonizer 11,000 years ago.

Q. How many species of cactus are there in Death Valley?
   A) 13   B) 33   C) 113
A. A) Only 13. The valley floor is too hot and dry for cactus, and the mountains are too cold.

Q. The arrowweed is the plant that makes up the Devils Cornfield. How did the arrowweed get its name?
   A) It's shaped like an arrow.
   B) Native Americans used it to make arrows.
   C) It has a poison as deadly as an arrow.
A. B) The Timbisha Shoshones used its strong, stiff stems to make arrows.

Q. The most noticeable plant at the Salt Creek Interpretative Trail is the pickleweed, the plant with the segmented stems. What does the pickleweed have in common with the pupfish that live in Salt Creek?
A. A very high tolerance for salt. The ground here is saturated

---

Devils Hole pupfish can live in water up to 100 F (37.8 C).

with salt, too much for most plants. The pickleweed is also called the Iodine bush; both names give you a clue about how it tastes.

Q. In Death Valley a plant's distribution is often determined by its ability to withstand salt. After the creosote bush, the most common shrub in Death Valley is the desert holly, which isn't a real holly, but a salt bush. It can tolerate salt much better than creosotes can, so you'll see it growing at the edge of the salt pan. Some plants can grow right on the salt pan. If the salt content of the soil is less than 0.5 percent, mesquite will grow. If the salt content is between 0.5 percent and 3 percent, you'll find arrowweed. Between 3 percent and 6 percent, pickleweed grows. What will grow above 6 percent salt content?
A. Nothing at all.

Q. The desert holly has a white tinge to it. What gives it this color?
   A) Salt   B) Dirt   C) Fungus
A. A) Salt. The desert holly absorbs salt from the soil and uses it to coat its leaves. The white reflects the sun and helps keep the plant cooler. The holly's leaves point up at a 70-degree angle, which minimizes exposure to the midday sun. Other Death Valley plants have other sun-avoidance strategies, such as small leaves, tightly curled leaves, waxy leaves, leaves that drop off in summer, or leaves covered with tiny hairs. The rock nettle's hairs are so sharp that leaves will stick to human clothing and skin, giving the rock nettle the nickname "the velcro plant."

Q. How old are the bristlecone pine trees on the Panamint Mountains?
   A) 300 years old   B) 750 years   C) 3,000 years
A. C) Up to 3,000 years old. North of Death Valley, a bristlecone pine has been found to be about 4,800 years old—it's the oldest living thing on Earth (unless you count the creosote bushes that survive by cloning).

Q. Wildflower blooms in Death Valley can be spectacular. But the blooms depend on rainfall, which varies greatly from year to

---

Even in Death Valley, some people have allergic reactions to wildflowers.

year. What kind of rainfall will produce a better wildflower bloom: light rains spread out all fall and winter, or the same amount of rain for one week in early February?

A. Light rains all fall and winter. Plants need to store up a lot of nutrients and water to produce a crop of wildflowers, and they can't afford to waste their flowers and seeds on ground that is too dry. Seeds are "programmed" to recognize if there was enough rain—they have a chemical coating that gradually washes off in the rain. If there hasn't been enough rain by February, plants have already called it quits and will wait for a better year.

Q. When do wildflowers bloom in Death Valley?
A. On the valley floor and alluvial fans, the wildflower bloom is best from mid-February to mid-April. From 2,000 feet (610 m) to 4,000 feet (1,219 m), which includes the passes into Death Valley, the bloom goes from early April to early May. Up in the Panamint Mountains, flowers are still blooming in early June.

Q. What's the most common wildflower in Death Valley?
A. The wildflower scene in Death Valley is dominated by one yellow flower, the desertgold. Yes, desertgold is its real name. The desertgold is a member of the sunflower family. It grows up to two feet tall. Even in a dry year you'll start seeing some by mid-February, and in a wet year they truly turn the desert golden.

Q. How did the "gravel ghost" flower get its name?
A. The flower (white, about one inch wide) sits atop a very thin, leafless stem, which can be so hard to see that the flower appears to be floating in thin air. It grows in the gravel beds of drainages.

Plants with high salt tolerance are called "halophytes,"
Greek for "salt + plant."

HISTORY
49ERS, MINERS, 20-MULE
TEAMS, GHOST TOWNS

"There is a story in every canyon, a novel in every league of Death Valley."

—Father John J. Crowley

Q. The Death Valley 49ers were a group of pioneers heading for the California gold fields during the 1849 gold rush. They were mostly from the Midwest and South, regions that gave them little preparation for surviving in the desert. They ended up in America's worst desert because they were trying to avoid the opposite extreme. They arrived in Salt Lake City too late in the year of 1849 to avoid the snows in the Sierra Nevada Mountains.

Only three years previously, a wagon train got trapped in the Sierra snow, with a result that became famous. What was it?
A. The Donner party ran out of food and resorted to cannibalism. In trying to avoid the fate of the Donner party, the 49ers became just as famous for a desert survival ordeal.

Q. From Salt Lake City, the 49ers headed southwest on the Old Spanish Trail, which would lead them to Los Angeles. But since the gold fields were to the west, the 49ers became impatient and decided to follow a rumor that there was a short cut to the west. The 49ers didn't understand that in Basin and Range country, the mountains run north-south, so if you try going straight west, you have to cross the mountains. When they told their guide, Jefferson Hunt, that they were leaving the trail for this short cut, what did Hunt say?

   A) "Go west, young man."
   B) "This trail is long and dusty, but long proven."
   C) "I believe you will get into the jaws of hell."
A. C) "I believe you will get into the jaws of hell."

Q. The best-known of the 49ers is William Manly, whose book about his ordeal, *Death Valley in '49*, is one of the classics of the American frontier. As the 49ers advanced, they split into several groups and tried different routes. When Manly's group realized they were lost in the desert with little food or water, they sent Manly and John Rogers to find the way and bring help, while the others remained at a spring. Manly and Rogers had to go over 200 miles (321 km) before they found a ranch, then they had to repeat that distance to get back to Death Valley. How long did this roundtrip take?
   A) 10 days   B) 18 days   C) 26 days

The last of the Death Valley 49ers died in 1923.

A. C) 26 days. Manly called it "a struggle which seemed almost hopeless."

Q. William Manly also became famous for another feat of exploration on his way to Death Valley. What was it?

A) He climbed Pikes Peak.

B) He boated down the Green River in Utah.

C) He discovered Mt. Rushmore.

A. B) Manly became one of the first Americans to boat down the Green River. Manly was hoping the Green River was a short cut to California, but as with Death Valley, Manly had no idea of where he was going. The Green River was full of dangerous rapids. After getting knocked overboard and being warned by Indians about worse rapids ahead, Manly quit the Green River. He would go from nearly drowning in Utah to nearly dying of thirst in Death Valley.

"The hardest thing on the whole trip was not the gnawing hunger or the burning thirst. It was not the rough rocky road or the burning fatigue. It was not the sorrow of watching companions die or the anxious uncertainty of what the next day would bring. The hardest thing was hearing the pitiful cries of my child, asking for a drink of water, and I having none to give him. Sometimes at night I can hear those cries in my mind, and it still tears my heart."

—Juliet Brier, Death Valley 49er

And yet, on Christmas Day Juliet Brier and her husband, who were on their own in Death Valley, found a small stream, which saved their lives. That night they became the first Americans to celebrate Christmas in Death Valley. They killed one of their oxen and had meat for dinner, and coffee, and a bit of their last bread. They enjoyed a bath too.

Q. When the 49ers were going hungry in Death Valley, they came upon a mysterious substance and supposed it was a stash of Indian food. William Manly described it as "balls of a glistening substance looking like pieces of variegated candy stuck together. The balls were as large as small pumpkins. It was evidently food of some sort and we found it sweet but sickish, and those who

---

A basic prospector food was hardtack, a hard bread.

were so hungry as to break up one of the balls...making a good meal of it, were a little troubled with nausea afterward." What were they really eating?

    A) Indian candy   B) Pack rat urine   C) Mineral deposits

A. B) Pack rat urine, which solidifies into hard, shiny globs.

Q. How many 49ers died in Death Valley?

    A) Only one   B) 87   C) 125

A. A) Only one, 48-year-old Richard Culverwell. Luckily, the 49ers were there in December, so it wasn't hot. But the name "Death Valley" cast such a spell that legends soon sprang up that dozens or hundreds of 49ers had died.

Q. Of the 26 covered wagons the 49ers drove into Death Valley, how many wagons made it through?

    A) Only one   B) 12   C) 24

A. Only one, driven by Harry Wade, who saw the logic of avoiding the north-south mountains by heading south. All the other wagons were abandoned. Harry Wade later went into the freighting business.

Q. True or false: The wagon tracks of the 49ers were still visible ten years later.

A. True. The lack of rain helped preserve them. Also, desert soils are especially sensitive to compression. Archaeologists have studied the old mining areas in Death Valley and found that even a year or two of human activities left the soil so compressed that plant growth has still not recovered after a century. Today on the Scotty's Castle Road you can see century-old wagon tracks on the old road between Rhyolite and Skidoo.

Jefferson Hunt, who warned the 49ers against leaving the Old Spanish Trail...

Q. True or false: A trunk the 49ers left in a cave was discovered in 1998.

A. False. A trunk was indeed found, but it turned out to be a hoax. Some of the items inside didn't fit a date of 1849. For example, a ceramic bowl said "Made in Germany," but Germany wasn't founded until 1871.

Q. Did the Death Valley 49ers ever find any gold?

A. After all their troubles, the 49ers failed to find gold, and most returned home. William Rood, after surviving the desert, drowned in the Colorado River at Yuma in 1870. Charles Arcan, only eleven years old in 1849, could never get enough water: he became a champion swimmer and swimming coach. Harry Wade, the only 49er to get out of Death Valley with his wagon, committed suicide in 1883.

> The Death Valley 49ers have become icons of the American West. In some respects, this is surprising. It's not as if they blazed an important trail or founded a city. All they did was blunder into Death Valley, and survive it. But America's sense of identity has long been based on the pioneering of a huge continent, by those who succeeded through bravery, suffering, and toughness. In Death Valley, the pioneers encountered the toughest of tests, and passed. Death Valley has continued being a theater of American national mythology, with its stories of prospectors, 20-mule teams, Death Valley Scotty's self-mythologizing, and TV's *Death Valley Days*.

Q. It turned out that there was gold in Death Valley. How did Death Valley gold prospecting and mining compare with other famous gold rushes?

A. It was half a century after the 1849 California gold rush that gold was discovered in Death Valley. Meanwhile, there was the Pikes Peak gold rush in Colorado in 1857, and the Klondike gold rush in 1896. The first big gold rush in the desert Southwest didn't start until 1900, in Tonopah-Goldfield, Nevada. A few years before that, gold was found just outside Death Valley, at Ballarat. In 1904 the Bullfrog gold rush (around Rhyolite) began. The other significant Death Valley gold strikes (Harrisburg, Skidoo, and the Keane

---

...later founded the city of San Bernardino, California.

Wonder Mine) also happened around this time. But compared with gold strikes like Pikes Peak or Tonopah-Goldfield, Death Valley's gold deposits were modest, and were mined out in a few years.

Q. There was a great deal of prospecting for precious metals in and around Death Valley, but only about a hundred claims turned out to be worth mining, and only a half-dozen claims were truly rich. This was out of a total of how many mining claims in Death Valley?

   A) 500   B) 1,000   C) 20,000

A. C) 20,000.

> The three richest gold mines in Death Valley (in 1910 dollars—it's over 20 times this much in today's dollars):
> Montgomery Shoshone (Rhyolite) $1.4 million
> Skidoo $1.3 million
> Keane Wonder $1.0 million

Q. For over 30 years after 1849, prospectors looking for silver and gold in Death Valley were making footprints in a substance that turned out to be worth more than all the gold, silver, and other precious metals in Death Valley combined. What was it?

A. Borax.

Q. Archaeologists can often determine the exact years that prospectors used a camp, not just in Death Valley but throughout the American West. What artifact is used most often for this?

   A) Newspapers left in a camp
   B) Dates carved on rocks
   C) Bottles and cans

A. C) Bottles and cans. Just like today, the shapes and materials of beer bottles and food cans changed every few years. Archaeologists recognize these changing styles, just like they use the changing styles of Native American pottery. Especially useful are condensed-milk cans, a favorite item of cowboys and miners. Archaeologists carry charts that show all the changing styles of condensed-milk cans, allowing them to date a campsite to within a few years.

The Lost Burro Mine was discovered by a prospector looking for his lost burro.

Q. Prospectors depended on their burros, especially in Death Valley. Burros could go without water, and could smell water from a long distance, sometimes saving the lives of prospectors. Many prospectors became so loyal to their burros that they would go hungry and feed their last food to their burros. Shorty Borden, who had a mine high up on the Panamint Mountains, worried that his favorite burro, Hanaupah Jack, was getting too chilly. Borden went into Lone Pine and bought a present for Hanaupah Jack. But the wild burros who were usually happy to greet Hanaupah Jack didn't like his new present, and they ran away when they saw him coming. What was Hanaupah Jack's present?

A. A flannel bathrobe. Shorty Borden had to do a bit of adjusting to make it fit a burro, and he tied it on with a belt of rope.

Q. Many prospectors spent many years in Death Valley and never found anything, but some of the richest mines were discovered through dumb luck. The richest silver strike, at Panamint City, was discovered by two robbers looking for a hiding place. One of the richest gold mines, Skidoo, was discovered through what unusual circumstance?

A) Two prospectors got lost in a fog

B) A psychic predicted its location

C) An airplane pilot saw something glittering below

A. A) Death Valley almost never has fog, but in 1906 two prospectors got lost in a fog, went up the wrong canyon, and struck gold.

Q. The Wells Fargo Company was usually eager to establish stage coach service to booming mining towns, since hauling silver and gold was very profitable. The only time in its history that Wells Fargo refused to establish stage coach service to a mining boomtown was to Panamint City. The Panamint City mine was owned by Nevada's U.S. Senator William M. Stewart, who as an attorney had worked for Wells Fargo, but even he couldn't persuade Wells Fargo to open a stage coach line. Why did they refuse?

In Shoshone, just outside Death Valley, miners lived in caves, which can be seen today.

A. Panamint City lay at the end of a series of long, narrow canyons, which were full of perfect ambush spots for robbers. Panamint City itself lay in such a narrow canyon that the town was a mile (1.6 km) long, but had no side streets. In 1876 a flash flood wiped out much of the town.

Q. Senator Stewart came up with a way to transport his silver and avoid robberies. What was it?
 A) He shipped it with 12 armed guards.
 B) He shipped it by hot-air balloon.
 C) He cast the silver into 750-pound (340 kg) balls, too heavy for anyone to steal.

A. C) He cast it into 750-pound (340 kg) balls. At least, this is the legend. One reliable source says they were 400-pound (181 kg) squares. In any case, they were too heavy for robbers on horses to lift or to ride off with.

Q. One study of violence in the Wild West compared various towns that were famous for their violence. Which place was the most violent?
 A) Dodge City   B) Tombstone
 C) Deadwood   D) Panamint City

A. D) Panamint City. In Dodge City's deadliest year (1878) there were five killings. In Deadwood's deadliest year (1876) there were four killings—including Wild Bill Hickok. In Tombstone's deadliest year (1881) there were five killings. But in 1874-75, Panamint City recorded five killings in only five months. In Panamint City's isolation, miners entertained themselves with drinking and gambling, which led to many personal conflicts.

Q. The gold town of Skidoo was named for the early 1900s slang term "23 skidoo," which means "scram." Why did it get this name?
 A) Skidoo got its water from a 23-mile (37 km) long pipeline from Telescope Peak.
 B) Skidoo was discovered on the 23rd day of the month.
 C) Skidoo started out as 23 mining claims.
 D) Someone thought it was a fun name.

A. You can find all these explanations in various history books.

The Ashford brothers hired a spiritualist to find gold. It didn't work.

Skidoo Mine

This is a good example of how Death Valley history has faded into legends over the years. Prospectors didn't have a lot of entertainment, so they enjoyed spinning legends and claiming credit, which hasn't made things easy for historians.

Q. The richest gold strike in the Death Valley area, the Bullfrog district, named for the green tint of its ore, was discovered by prospector Shorty Harris. Shorty Harris never got much benefit from his discoveries. After discovering Bullfrog, Shorty went into town to celebrate, and when he woke up the next morning he found that he had signed away his claim, worth millions. How much had he gotten for it?

    A) $1,000   B) $10,000   C) $25,000

A. A) $1,000, and he soon spent most of that buying drinks for his friends. A few years later Shorty made another major gold find, which was even named for him, Harrisburg. But before filing a claim on it, Shorty went into town and bragged about it, and other prospectors rushed to the site and claimed most of it.

> "Who the hell wants $10,000,000? It's the game, man—the game."
>
> —Shorty Harris

Q. Almost everything used in Death Valley mining towns had to be brought in from far away, making things very expensive. In the

---

When miners at the Keane Wonder Mine drilled a well for water, they struck more gold.

1906 boomtown of Greenwater, how much did a gallon of gas cost? (These figures are adjusted into today's dollars).

   A) $10   B) $15   C) $20

A. C) $20. In spite of the town's name, it wasn't very green, and had little water. Water was brought in and sold at $2 per gallon. A breakfast of ham and eggs cost $20.

Compared to Greenwater's costs, the high cost of transporting materials to Death Valley turned into a bargain for one gold mill. When the Ashford mill was being built in 1915, its owners ordered one railroad car of cement, but the cement company accidentally shipped two railroad cars of cement. When the cement company calculated how much it would cost to have the extra cement shipped back, they decided it was cheaper to let the Ashford mill keep all the cement. This is why the Ashford mill foundations have unusually thick cement walls.

Q. Swinging a miner's pick all day took a lot of muscle power. One early Death Valley miner, Walter Hoover, had a unique preparation for mining. It was:

   A) He'd run a weight-training gym.
   B) He'd won the world championship in rowing.
   C) As a door-to-door salesman, he'd carried heavy Hoover vacuum cleaners.

A. B) He'd won a famous rowing competition on the Thames River, which was considered the world championship.

The popular image of the western prospector is of a tough, whiskered, old coot, but there were at least a dozen women prospectors in Death Valley. Historian Sally Zanjani researched women prospectors in the West for her book *A Mine of Her Own* and found that Death Valley had the largest group of women prospectors. Lillian Malcolm appeared in several Broadway plays in 1896-97, rushed off to the Klondike gold rush, then came to Death Valley to prospect. Panamint Annie, whose real name was Mary Elizabeth White, came to Death Valley in 1934 after being diagnosed with tuberculosis. Panamint Annie loved Death Valley for its own sake, say-

A dozen Death-Valley-area towns published newspapers...

ing: "The desert...moves just like waves in the ocean." The most successful Death Valley woman prospector was Louise Grantham, who studied education at USC and came to Death Valley to track down a prospector who had accepted a grub-stake from Louise's father, then disappeared. When Louise found the prospector she had to use her gun to force him to surrender the truck and grub he had bought. She went into prospecting for herself and found a rich talc deposit, which she mined for the next 50 years. One of the most popular episodes of *Death Valley Days* was "Claim Jumpin' Jennie." Jennie wasn't really a claim jumper; she worked hard at prospecting to put her daughter through school.

Q. "Dad" Fairbanks was a longtime Death Valley area prospector and merchant who is still remembered for all the people he rescued in the desert. After prospecting for 35 years, he finally struck it rich in an unlikely way. What was it?

A) He shot at a rabbit and struck oil.

B) He saw a Shoshone Indian woman washing her hair.

C) He won the lottery.

A. B) He saw a Shoshone woman washing her hair in a pan filled with something that looked like buttermilk. It was a clay mixture that served to filter out dirt, and it did wonders for her hair. Fairbanks found the source of this clay and filed a claim on it. In the early days of the oil industry, clays were used to filter heavier oils. A Death Valley clay mining boom followed, including a miners camp called "Clay City."

Prospecting in Death Valley involved quite a bit of foolishness and greed, but it also offered the American Dream, rewarding ordinary people and honest hard work with success. A good example of this is Pete Aguereberry, a Basque who emigrated to America at age 15 without speaking a word of English. Pete spent his first three years in America herding sheep, but lots of things went wrong, including 1,500 of his sheep stampeding over a cliff, so for three years of work Pete earned only $10. Pete didn't start out as a frontiersman: when he first saw a skunk he thought it was a pretty cat and tried to pet it; the skunk was not amused. One day

...the most famous was the Death Valley Chuck-Walla, *named for the big lizard.*

Pete couldn't understand why his bedroll was rattling—he had rolled up a rattlesnake inside it! Pete tried many jobs, but things always seemed to go wrong. Driving a stage coach, he got caught in a blizzard and nearly froze. He worked hauling water, but his boss cheated him out of his wages. When Pete first tried prospecting, he thought he'd struck it rich, but he'd only struck fool's gold. Then he passed up a claim he thought was worthless, and it soon made a fortune for someone else. Finally, when he was crossing the Panamints on his way to a 4th of July celebration, he found a vein of gold, the Eureka mine, which he worked for the next 35 years. It didn't make him rich, but he was happy to make a steady living from it. In his spare time Pete built a road to a Death Valley overlook, just so strangers could enjoy the view. This overlook is now called Aguereberry Point.

When World War Two started, a Death Valley miner named Buck Johnson tried to enlist in the Marines, but he was turned down because he was 45 years old. Buck wrote to President Roosevelt pointing out that the Marines needed explosives experts—like Buck. The Marines enlisted him. During a combat landing on a South Pacific island, a low tide caused some landing craft to get stuck on a coral reef. The Marines sent in Buck, who blew a passage in the reef. Buck was awarded a Silver Star.

Mill at Keane Wonder Mine

Q. The Keane Wonder Mine was a "wonder" partly for its aerial tramway for carrying gold ore from the mine, high up a cliff, to the mill below. The tramway stretched nearly a mile (1.6 km) and dropped 1,400 feet (426 m). A series of towers, as tall as 35 feet (11 m), held a cable and 22 buckets. Each bucket had a 600-pound (272 kg) capacity. The buckets arrived at the bottom every two minutes. To

20-mule-team mules were insured for $10,000 each...

Lost Mines of Death Valley

A lost mine is a rich lode of ore that someone found but that no one was able to find again. Since Death Valley is a large, confusing place and early travelers didn't have maps or know where they were, it's plausible that a discovery might be lost. On the other hand, some were probably only legends, such as the Lost Bullet Mine, where Indians supposedly made bullets out of gold.

The Lost Gunsight mine: One of the Death Valley 49ers broke the gunsight on his rifle and replaced it with a slice of rock he picked up. Later he took his gun to a gunsmith and was told that the slice of rock was pure silver.

The Lost Breyfogle mine: In 1865 prospector Charles Brey-fogle was found lying nearly dead in the desert. He was carrying some incredibly rich gold ore, but he had become so lost and delirious that he couldn't recall where he got it. For years Breyfogle returned to Death Valley to search, but he never found more gold. The term "Breyfogling" became a common word throughout the West for searching for lost treasure.

The Lost Chinaman mine: In the 1880s a Chinese worker quit the borax works in Death Valley and headed across the desert. Along the way he found some rich gold and took along a piece. But his trek was so terrible that he died soon after reaching a town.

The Lost Goller mine: Another Death Valley 49er, John Goller, was leaving Death Valley through the Panamint Mountains when he found some gold nuggets in a creek bed. People searched for this source for years, leaving them wondering if the gold had been covered by a flash flood.

...drivers earned $125 per month.

process so much ore, there was a large mill with heavy "stamps" to crush the ore. Each stamp weighed about 1,000 pounds (453 kg). How fast did the stamps hit the ore?

A) Once a minute   B) 10 times a minute
C) 100 times a minute

A. C) 100 times a minute. It was very noisy! But this wasn't the end of the process. The stamp mill could extract only 60 percent of the gold from the ore. Next, ore was dissolved in vats of cyanide, which extracted about 90 percent of the gold. The use of toxic chemicals like cyanide is one reason why old mining sites can be dangerous.

> "The palpable sense of mystery in the desert air breeds fables, chiefly of lost treasure...it is a question whether it is not better to be bitten by the little horned snake...than by the tradition of a lost mine."
> —Mary Austin, *Land of Little Rain*

Q. A few of Death Valley's most famous mines didn't have any ore; they were outright hoaxes, designed to trick east-coast investors into buying mining stocks. The most notorious Death Valley swindle was Greenwater, a copper claim that promoters promised would become "the richest mineral producing city on the whole globe." In four months in 1906 investors poured in $30 million. A town sprang up, and a thousand miners flocked in. By the time the bubble had burst, what was the total worth of all the ore taken from Greenwater?

A) $2,625   B) $252,625   C) $2 million

A. A) $2,625—and nine cents. Greenwater was called the mining swindle of the century.

Q. Another mining swindle was Leadfield, which did have some lead, but not enough to justify the grandiose claims C. C. Julian made for it. Julian rented a train to bring hundreds of investors from Los Angeles to Leadfield for a big promotional show. His publicity flyer showed steamboats on the Amargosa River: can you spot anything wrong with *that* image?

A. The Amargosa River is almost always dry.

Rhyolite's train station cost $130,000, and was abandoned after ten years.

Q. Death Valley has more abandoned mines than any other national park. How many?

A) 500   B) 1,000   C) 6,000

A. C) 6,000, at least. There are so many abandoned mines that the National Park Service hasn't been able to count them all. There may be as many as 10,000.

Q. Abandoned mines may have some of the romance of ghost towns, but they can be very dangerous. Why?

A) When mines were abandoned, miners removed the timber supports, so mines easily cave in.

B) Mines have vertical shafts, down which people can fall.

C) The air deep inside mines is bad, even poisonous.

D) Toxic chemicals used in milling are still present.

E) All of the above

A. E) All of the above

Rhyolite bank

Q. In Death Valley even the ghost towns are ghostly: there's often almost nothing left except for debris on the ground. What happened to the buildings?

A. Lumber was scarce in Death Valley, so when a town was abandoned, people soon hauled the wood to other places. Entire buildings were moved. The Presbyterian church in Rhyolite was moved to Ryan to serve as a community building. One Rhyolite resident went away for a few weeks and returned to discover that someone had hauled his house away. Many buildings from Greenwater were hauled to Shoshone.

Five Death Valley **ghost towns** where the past lives:

1. Rhyolite. The best-preserved ghost town is also the easiest to reach. Includes walls of a 3-story bank, a house made of beer bottles, and a train station.

2. Leadfield. Getting there is more than half the fun, as Leadfield is on the spectacular Titus Canyon road. A few

Rhyolite had a pet burro who got food handouts at all the cafes.

buildings remain, and lots of (dangerous) tunnels.

3. Skidoo. Like many Death Valley ghost towns, there's not much left to see here, mainly lots of junk on the ground. But it's not junk to archaeologists; it's valuable historical evidence, protected by law.

4. Wildrose charcoal kilns. The echo inside the 25-foot (8 m) tall kilns sure sounds ghostly. Built in 1877, these are the best-preserved charcoal kilns in the West.

5. Eureka Mine. Pete Aguereberry's mine, equipment, house, furniture, and cars are right where he left them on his death in 1945.

Q. Rhyolite (named for a type of volcanic rock) was founded in late 1904. By 1908 it had an estimated population of 10,000. What was its population in the 1910 census?
    A) 25,675   B) 2,675   C) 675
A. C) 675. In the 1920 census, it was only 16. Rhyolite disappeared because the gold ore of the Bullfrog district was depleted. In its peak year, 1908, Bullfrog produced $600,000 worth of gold. Three years later, it produced only $46,000. At its peak Rhyolite had 270 school-age kids and built a $20,000 school, but by the time the school opened, there weren't enough kids left in Rhyolite to fill one room.

"Everywhere lie ruin and debris, and as you pick your way amid scattered timbers and rusted iron the black eyes of abandoned tunnels gaze unblinkingly at you from the hills, watchdogs of a ghost town which once knew hope and despair, truth and falsehood, life and death. Leadfield is no more, but it is still a splendid spot for meditation on the vanity of human glory."

—Father John J. Crowley

Q. Lumber may have been in short supply in Rhyolite, but there were plenty of discarded beer bottles. One man used them to build a house. How many bottles are in his house?

Wildrose Charcoal Kilns produced fuel for processing silver/lead ore.

A) 5,000   B) 30,000   C) 50,000

A. B) 30,000 is the official count, though some sources claim more. Some bottles still contain dried beer foam. Most bottles are stamped "AB," for Adolphus Busch.

> Joke: What's the easiest way to find rusty nails in a ghost town?
> Answer: With your tires.

Q. The Wildrose charcoal kilns were built in 1877 by George Hearst, the father of newspaper magnate William Randolph Hearst, who was the subject of the classic movie *Citizen Kane*, a movie about the bad consequences of greed. The Wildrose kilns were built to supply charcoal to the ore smelter at Hearst's Modoc mine 29 miles (46 km) away. The kilns made charcoal out of pinyon trees. Pinyon trees take many decades to grow and their nutritious pine nuts had kept Death Valley's Native Americans alive for a thousand years. When miners began cutting down the pinyon trees, a few Native Americans launched an attack, but it was hopeless. How long did the mine last?

A) 3 years   B) 50 years   C) 100 years

A. A) Only three years. Then the ore was gone, and so were many thousands of pinyon trees, and so was the ancient way of life of the Timbisha Shoshone.

Q. Eager to find gold, the 49ers drove their wagons right over Death Valley's "white gold"—borax. They thought it was just ordinary salt. Who finally discovered that it was a lot more valuable?

A. In 1881 Aaron and Rosie Winters were living a hardscrabble life at Ash Meadows, just east of Death Valley. A prospector came by looking for borax, told them what it looked like, and showed them how to perform a chemical test for it. Aaron remembered the salt beds in Death Valley, and he quickly went there, performed the test, and realized it was no ordinary salt.

Timbisha Shoshones watched the 49ers struggle through Death Valley.

Q. What's the leading use of borax?
A) Soaps and detergents
B) Glass, including fiberglass insulation
C) Ceramics and enamels, including the tiles on NASA's Space Shuttle
D) Plant fertilizers
E) Play-Doh and Silly Putty

A. B) 43 percent of borax use is for glass, including Pyrex, crystals, and fiberglass insulation. Borax is most famous as a soap, but this amounts to 17 percent of its use. Ceramics and enamels, including the heat-resistant tiles on the space shuttle, account for 12 percent; plant fertilizers are 5 percent; and 23 percent is for other uses, including flame retardants, circuit boards, medicines, automotive fluids, and yes, Play-Doh and Silly Putty.

Q. The Harmony Borax Works began operation in 1882, mining and processing borax on the floor of Death Valley for shipment by 20-mule teams. Most of the laborers were of one nationality. Which?
A) Irish   B) Chinese   C) Welsh

A. B) Chinese. They were paid $1.30 per day—actually a good wage for the 1880s. It had to be a good wage or no one would tolerate the tough conditions and back-breaking labor. The Chinese

workers also used sledge hammers to break a wagon road through the Devils Golf Course. (The salt formations have grown back, so no trace of this road remains today.) Chinese workers also built much of the railroad tracks in the American West.

Q. The Harmony Borax Works shut down in the summer months. Why?
A) Concern for the health of workers

Salt mines in the Saline Valley used a tramway to lift salt...

B) Not enough water

C) It was too hot for the borax to be processed

A. C) Borax had to crystallize in large vats, but too much heat prevented the crystals from forming.

Q. For a while, Death Valley had another borax works, the Eagle Borax Works, developed by Mr. Isadore Daunet. The first time Daunet came to Death Valley, he and his companions got lost and ran out of water. Two of his companions died. What did Daunet do to survive?

A) He dug a hole to find water.

B) He lit a signal fire.

C) He killed his pack animals and drank their blood.

A. C) Daunet killed his pack animals and drank their blood. Four years later, after Daunet had set up his borax works, the price of borax fell and he went bankrupt. He put a gun to his head and shot himself.

Q. The most famous mules of the American West are the mules of the Death Valley 20-mule teams of the 1880s, and the mules that carry riders to the bottom of the Grand Canyon. Which job killed more mules?

A) Death Valley   B) Grand Canyon

C) No mules died in either job.

A. C) No mules ever died in either job. Mules are tough and smart animals. Mules were used in Death Valley instead of horses because mules can do more work, go longer without water, they are smarter, and they get a better look at where they are placing their feet, which is important on rough, steep climbs. While prospectors used burros for their relatively modest loads, mules can pull far more weight than burros.

Q. How many mules were on a 20-mule team?

A. You thought this one would be easy, didn't you? There were a total of 20 animals, but only 18 were mules. Two horses were placed closest to the front wagon, since the horses' greater weight helped in turning the wagons. The phrase "20-mule team" was an advertising slogan for the Borax Company, and of course, advertising slogans tend to oversimplify things.

...thousands of feet over the Inyo mountains.

Q. Mules were smart enough to understand the shouted commands of their drivers. But one morning one driver just couldn't get his mules to start pulling. What was wrong?

   A) It was too windy for the mules to hear.
   B) The mules were on strike for more hay.
   C) The driver had decided to become a Christian.

A. C) The driver had just heard a preacher preach against the evils of swearing, so the driver omitted the swear words he usually used in his commands. The mules were so accustomed to the swear words, they didn't know what to do.

Q. True or false: The mules of the 20-mule teams were required to dance.

A. True. "The Dance of the Mules" was a maneuver required for turning sharp bends. If all the mules were pulling at an angle, they could pull the wagons off the road, or even tip them over. To prevent this, a few mules near the wagons were trained to jump over the pulling chain and pull away from the direction of the turn. When the wagons had safely accomplished the turn, these mules jumped back over the chain.

Q. How far did the 20-mule teams haul their wagons?

   A) 16 miles (27 km)   B) 82 miles (131 km)
   C) 165 miles (265 km)

A. C) 165 miles (265 km), from Death Valley to the town of Mojave, which was on the railroad. A round-trip was 330 miles (531 km), and took three weeks. They averaged 16–18 miles (26–29 km) per day. Two 50-mile (80 km) stretches didn't have springs, which was why the mules also hauled a large water tank. In hotter weather, the teams might travel at night.

Q. Even before the borax wagons were loaded with ore, they were heavy. How much did a borax wagon weigh?

   A) 2,000 pounds (907 kg)   B) 5,200 pounds (2,358 kg)
   C) 7,800 pounds (3,538 kg)

A. C) 7,800 pounds (3,538 kg). A borax wagon was made of thick wood, and was sixteen feet (4.8 m) long, four feet (1.2 m) wide, and six feet (1.8 m) deep. The rear wheels were seven feet (2.1 m) tall; the front wheels were five feet (1.5 m) tall; and wheels

―――――――――――――――――――

While no mules died on the 20-mule teams...

had steel "tires" eight inches (20 cm) wide and one inch (2.5 cm) thick.

Q. When a wagon was loaded with ore, it weighed 31,800 pounds (14,424 kg). When you linked two wagons and a water tank that held 1,200 gallons (4,542 L), the entire wagon train weighed 73,000 pounds (33,112 kg). This was over twice the weight of the mules on the 20-mule team. This 73,000 pounds (33,112 kg) was equal to how many African elephants?

  A) 2   B) 3   C) 5

A. C) 5. One 20-mule team was pulling the weight of five African elephants across 165 miles (265 km) of hot desert, sometimes uphill.

Q. The 20-mule teams hauled borax out of Death Valley for only five years. Then the Borax Company found sources of borax nearer to the railroad. In those five years, the 20-mule teams hauled approximately 20 million pounds (9,000 metric tons) of borax. What would this weight amount to in the weight of Boeing 747s?

  A) 5 Boeing 747s   B) 25   C) 50

A. C) About 50. Those mules pulled borax equal to the weight of 50 Boeing 747s across 165 miles (265 km) of hot desert. After borax mining in Death Valley ceased, the 20-mule teams continued hauling from other mines.

Q. How much was one 20-mule team load of borax worth, in today's money?

  A) $10,000   B) $25,000   C) $250,000

A. C) $250,000—a quarter of a million dollars.

...one driver murdered another.

Q. A few years after the 20-mule teams ceased operating, they began a new career as an advertising symbol for the Borax Company's soaps and detergents. As a symbol, the 20-mule teams embodied all the romance of the Wild West. Between 1900 and 1940, the 20-mule teams made four national promotional tours, which included the Rose Bowl parade, the St. Louis World's Fair, and a presidential inauguration. Starting in 1952 they were seen weekly on the *Death Valley Days* TV show. It was a 24-year-old Borax Company employee named Stephen Mather who got the idea of using the 20-mule team as an advertising symbol. Mather went on to an important career. What was it?

A) President of the Borax Company
B) First director of the National Park Service
C) An actor in the TV show *Leave It to Beaver*

A. B) First director of the National Park Service. Though the first national park was established in 1872, the National Park Service wasn't established until 1919. Just before then, Mather wrote a letter to the Secretary of the Interior complaining about how the parks were being managed. The Secretary replied that if Mather thought he could do better, he could become director of the National Park Service. As director, Mather set high standards for the parks.

Q. In front of Furnace Creek Ranch sits a steam tractor named "Dinah." Built in 1894, Dinah was supposed to replace the 20-mule teams, but Dinah wasn't as good as mules. What was wrong with Dinah?

A) Even on flat ground, Dinah got stuck in sand.
B) Dinah broke down constantly and required nightly work by a mechanic.
C) Dinah had a hard time climbing hills.
D) All of the above

A. D) All of the above. The mules got their jobs back, at least until the Borax Company built a railroad to its mine in Ryan. For a while, Dinah was used to haul ore from the Keane Wonder Mine to Beatty, but then Dinah broke down and sat abandoned in the desert for 20 years.

The whips used by 20-mule-team drivers were 28 feet (8.5 m) long.

Q. Was there ever a railroad in Death Valley?

A. No, not in the valley itself, but spurs of the Tonopah and Tidewater Railroad reached Ryan and Rhyolite, just outside today's park boundary. The Tonopah and Tidewater Railroad was named for the Nevada town of Tonopah and the tidewater of the Pacific Ocean, but the railroad never reached either place.

Q. Death Valley did have two other Wild West forms of transportation. For two years Death Valley had its own Pony Express, running from Panamint City to San Bernardino about 150  miles (241 km) away. When Rhyolite and Skidoo were thriving they were connected by a stage coach line. But these weren't the red Concord stage coaches familiar from western movies; they were "mud wagons" that weighed 1,000 pounds (450 kg) less than Concord stages, were easier on horses, and were less likely to bog down in mud (not a big problem in Death Valley)—or sand. In 1924 Death Valley had a form of transportation that was definitely *not* part of the Wild West. Decades later, it would be associated with Disneyland. What was it?

A. A monorail. It was used to haul Epsom salts through canyons so narrow and twisting that even a narrow gauge railroad wouldn't fit. The monorail was 28 miles (45 km) long and cost $200,000, but it was so plagued by mechanical troubles, and by a trestle collapse, that it bankrupted the mining company.

> "Fathomless beds of salt mark where its waters disappear. But, let us not forget that much of it is the salt of women's tears and the toil of honest men, many of whom have left their bones to bleach beneath these burning skies."
> —Father John J. Crowley

Until 1907 borax was used as a food preservative, but this wasn't safe.

Death Valley Tall Tales

Tall tales were always popular on the American frontier, and Death Valley's extreme conditions were perfect raw materials for them:

A prospector was crossing Death Valley in summer when he started choking. He spit into his hand and looked at a blob of gold. The gold filling in his tooth had melted.

A prospector's burro got a painful toothache and fled into the mountains. It came back with a solid gold filling in its tooth. The prospector spent years trying to find where the burro had chewed on gold ore to fill its cavity.

One July it was so hot that a prospector's supply of corn started popping, producing a big pile of popcorn. His burros thought it was snow and laid down in it—and froze to death.

Dan De Quille, a famous Virginia City, Nevada, humorist, told of an inventor who built a cooling machine for crossing Death Valley in summer, but the machine worked too well, and the inventor froze to death.

In 1907 the Rhyolite newspaper reported that a burro, sick of the heat, had committed suicide by banging its head against a rock.

The Rhyolite newspaper also announced the discovery of a "water mine," rocks so full of water that bighorn sheep ate them to get water.

Dan De Quille, born William Wright, was a failed prospector when he began a 30-year Nevada newspaper career that saw his essays published around the nation.

Since the Amargosa River often dries up, its fish have natural canteens attached to their tails. When the river dries up the fish tie themselves in a large hoop and roll over the desert in search of where the river still has water. This rolling stirs up lots of dust, which strangers imagine is a dust storm.

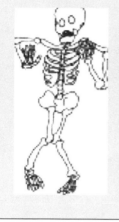

One miner had two problems: he needed ropes for mining, and his mine had too many rattlesnakes. He solved both problems by tying the rattlesnakes into ropes.

In a lonely shack two prospectors were sitting at a table when they got into an argument. They shot each other, and both died. Years later their skeletons were found still seated, pistols in bony hands, a pile of gold coins on the table.

The Amargosa River's water has a bitter taste from salts dissolved in it, so was named from the Spanish amargo, "bitter."

HISTORY
NATIVE AMERICANS,
TOURISTS, NATIONAL PARK

"If one is inclined to wonder at first how so many dwellers came to be in the loneliest land that ever came out of God's hands, what they do there and why they stay, one does not wonder so much after having lived there...The rainbow hills, the tender bluish mists, the luminous radiance of the spring, have the lotus charm."

—Mary Austin, *Land of Little Rain*

Q. The frenzy of mining in Death Valley was a fairly brief period in a long history of people who lived in and loved Death Valley for its own sake. First there were Native Americans, then visitors to

a national park. When did humans first inhabit Death Valley?
A. The earliest traces of humans are hunters' projectile points 11,000-12,000 years old. Projectile points can be dated because their shapes continued changing.

Q. What animals were hunted by Death Valley's first humans?
A. It was the end of the Ice Age and there were still huge animals like mammoths. More recently, the largest game animal was the desert bighorn sheep. Since waterfowl migrating across the desert had few choices about where to land, Native Americans built hunting blinds near springs. They also caught rabbits, coyotes, pack rats, and lizards—when you live in a desert, you can't be fussy.

Q. Did Native Americans do any farming in Death Valley?
A. Very little. There just wasn't enough water and good soil. But Native Americans were masters at making the most of naturally growing plants, using them not just for food but for medicines, baskets, clothing, dyes, and much more. The two most important food plants were mesquite beans, which grow on the valley floor, and pinyon pine nuts, which grow in the Panamint

Timbisha woman preparing pine nuts

Mountains. A pound of pinyon nuts has 2,800 calories, more than the 2,460 calories in a pound of Hershey's chocolate.

As Death Valley's climate has changed over the last 12,000 years, Native Americans have either adapted to it or left Death Valley for long periods. After the Ice Age, Death Valley gradually dried out, forcing its large animals to leave for other areas, and Native Americans left with them. By 5,000 years ago Native Americans were living around the many freshwater springs in Death Valley. They were still hunting, but they were also making better use of plants, as indicated by all the grinding stones they left. Unlike hunters,

The Shoshones are a large group of tribes in the Great Basin.

who always moved around, they were staying in one place long enough to justify building stone houses. But as these springs dried up, Native Americans had to choose between adapting to a desert climate or leaving, and they left. Around 2,000 years ago, during a wetter period, Native Americans returned, but as the climate dried again, they again gave up on Death Valley. About 1,000 years ago the Timbisha Shoshone arrived. They were masters of survival in the most extreme deserts, and they are still living in Death Valley today.

Q. "Timbisha" is the tribe's name for themselves. What does this term mean?

A. "Timbisha" refers to hematite, also called red ochre, a min-

eral used by Native Americans for painting rock art, pottery, and faces. This name has spiritual meanings, signifying healing and protection. But white settlers misunderstood this name and thought "Timbisha" was the tribe's name for Death Valley. The Timbisha Shoshones call Death Valley "Tupippuh," or "homeland." The Timbisha Shoshones were annoyed that whites called their homeland "Death Valley." This land has kept them alive for 1,000 years, and has spiritual meanings. Just because some fools blundered in, and didn't recognize the food right in front of their faces, wasn't a good reason to call it "Death Valley."

Timbisha mother and child

Q. Is there any rock art in Death Valley?

A. Quite a bit, mostly near water sources and game trails. Some boulders have been entirely covered with designs. There are also geoglyphs, rocks that have been arranged into large patterns on the ground. The longest geoglyph is 350 feet (106 m) long, and five are about 200 feet (61 m) long. They tend to be associated with water sources, as if they were prehistoric road signs pointing to water.

Q. The Timbisha Shoshone are famous for their baskets. Before

---

Ten per cent of the population of Inyo County (which includes Death Valley) is Native American.

Native Americans started making pottery, they used baskets for carrying and storing food. When baskets were treated with pine pitch, they could even hold water. Baskets had many ingenious uses, such as trapping rabbits. What did the Timbisha Shoshone use to make baskets?
    A) The twigs of willow trees
    B) The roots of cactus
    C) The bark of pinyon trees
A. A) The twigs of willow trees. By treating the willow twigs in various ways, such as by leaving on the bark, or by bleaching twigs in the sun, Native Americans obtained different colors. (Scotty's Castle has the park's best display of Timbisha Shoshone baskets.)

Q. Who was the first white settler in Death Valley?
A. In 1874 a Kentuckian named Andrew Jackson Laswell, sometimes called "Bellerin' Teck," started a ranch at today's Furnace Creek Ranch. He grew alfalfa for the livestock of miners.

Q. In the early 1900s Lou Beck became famous as "the good Samaritan of Death Valley." For years Beck and his dog, a Siberian bloodhound named Rufus, roamed the deserts in and around Death Valley doing something to save lives. What were they doing?
    A) Putting up signs   B) Taking water to dying travelers
    C) Finding gold and giving it to charity
A. A) Putting up signs pointing to water. It all started when Beck was prospecting in the desert and got lost and ran out of water. Beck was lying in the sand, expecting to die, when Rufus nudged him—with a wet nose! Rufus had found water. Beck survived, and he dedicated himself to helping travelers find water in the desert. At that time, when car travel was new, there were no public agencies responsible for putting up road signs. Beck started out making his own signs and walking through the desert to put them up. Rufus went along, wearing boots made of elk skin. Beck and Rufus got so much publicity that some supporters gave them a car to help them get around.

The Timbisha Shoshones lived in wickiups, made of willow branches...

In the 1920s and 1930s Death Valley had its own Saint Francis, a priest who dearly loved the desert, its creatures, and its people. Irish-born John J. Crowley was based at a church in Lone Pine but he ministered to a huge area that included Death Valley. His flock included many miners and other rough characters, but Crowley's gentle spirit soon won the respect of people of all faiths, or no faith. For years Crowley wrote a column for the Lone Pine newspaper, using the pen name "Inyokel," combining "Inyo County" and "yokel." This pen name allowed Father Crowley to write about subjects that might usually seem inappropriate for a priest. Crowley wrote about nature with wonder and celebration, and he encouraged appreciation of Death Valley. In 1940 Father Crowley was only 49 years old when he was killed in a car accident. He is honored by "Father Crowley Vista" on Highway 190, which includes a monument that says: "He passed this way."

Q. In 1937, to celebrate the opening of a new highway connecting Lone Pine and Death Valley, Father Crowley organized an elaborate ceremony that involved carrying something from Mt. Whitney to Badwater, from the highest point in the contiguous U.S. to the lowest point. This object was carried by nine forms of transportation that symbolized Death Valley history and human progress. This object started with an Indian runner, then was passed to a Pony Express rider, then a prospector, a covered wagon, a stage coach, a railroad, an automobile, and an airplane. When this object stayed in Lone Pine overnight, it was placed in the vault of the local bank by William Boyd, the actor who played Hopalong Cassidy. What was this object?

    A) A gold nugget   B) A gourd of water   C) A torch

A. B) A gourd of water, water taken from the highest lake in the Sierras and finally poured out at Badwater. This whole celebration was called "The Wedding of the Waters." When the gourd arrived at Badwater, signal fires were lit all the way to Mt. Whitney.

Q. The first road from Lone Pine to Death Valley was a toll road built in 1926 by Bob Eichbaum, who charged $2 per car, about $25 today. Eichbaum also built the first tourist lodging in Death Valley, Stovepipe Wells. Why is Stovepipe Wells located where it is?

...In winter, they built sturdier houses sunk into the ground.

A) It's at a natural spring.
B) It's on the first flat spot below the Panamint Mountains.
C) It's where the construction trucks broke down.

A. C) Stovepipe Wells lodge was supposed to be built at a spring called Stovepipe Well, which got its name when pioneers stuck a stovepipe in the spring to help travelers find it. But Bob Eichbaum's heavily loaded trucks got stuck in the sand four miles (6.4 km) before reaching the spring. Eichbaum unloaded his trucks and went ahead and built his lodge right where he was.

Q. In the 1940s Stovepipe Wells lodge was purchased by a man whose wife was world famous. Who was she?

  A) Amelia Earhart   B) Bette Davis   C) Eleanor Roosevelt

A. A) Amelia Earhart. After Earhart disappeared in 1937, her husband, George Putnam, remarried, and in 1947 he and his wife Peg bought Stovepipe Wells.

Q. The Panamint Springs lodge was built in 1937 by the niece of a famous Wild West hero. The builder's name was Agnes Cody Reid. Who was the hero?

A. Buffalo Bill Cody

Q. At many of the famous western national parks, tourist facilities were built by the big railroad companies, but not at Death Valley. Why was this?

A. Death Valley was a long way from a major railroad, and by the time it became a national monument in 1933, the era of railroad travel was winding down. In Death Valley most of the tourist facilities were built by the Borax Company, which was no longer mining borax there, and which saw the potential for tourism. But the Borax Company didn't foresee the age of automobile tourism, and at first they didn't even think of building a gas station in Death Valley.

Q. The Borax Company built Death Valley's luxury resort, the Furnace Creek Inn. The Inn's architect was Albert C. Martin, whose most famous building, now considered a classic of art deco style, is located in Los Angeles. What is it? (Hint: for years it appeared every week on the TV show *Dragnet*).

The park's oldest building is the Borax Museum, built in 1883...

A. The Los Angeles City Hall, the skyscraper that appears on the badge of the Los Angeles Police.

Q. How much did the original Furnace Creek Inn cost to build in 1927?

   A) $86,000   B) $1 million   C) $5 million

A. A) $86,000. The original lodge had only 12 rooms. The Borax Company wasn't confident that tourists would want to come to Death Valley. Over the next ten years, they added another 54 rooms. That $86,000 would be about $1 million in today's dollars.

Q. When Furnace Creek Inn first opened, it got some of its electricity from the same source as Scotty's Castle. What was it?

   A) It burned borax.   B) It burned coal.
   C) A waterwheel turned.

A. C) A Pelton waterwheel. Death Valley might seem like the last place where you'd rely on water power, but both Furnace Creek Inn and Scotty's Castle were near major springs. Later on, both places got diesel generators.

Q. There are huge palm trees at Furnace Creek Inn and Furnace Creek Ranch. Are these natural?

A. No, they were planted in the 1920s to provide shade and dates. For decades, dates were harvested and sold to tourists or used to make treats like date bread. But growing dates is very labor intensive, so it wasn't profitable. Coyotes and birds have continued eating the dates, thus spreading palm trees to distant springs. Date palms are very thirsty, so they were wiping out the native plants at these springs. Today the National Park Service eliminates palm trees that have invaded other areas.

Q. True or false: Death Valley has the only golf course in any national park.

A. True. It's at Furnace Creek Ranch, and it's 214 feet (65 m) be-

---

...and relocated from 20 Mule Team Canyon to
Furnace Creek Ranch in 1954.

low sea level. It's been rated as one of the 50 hardest golf courses in America, mainly because of the heat. Some golfers claim that due to the low elevation and high heat, golf balls don't fly as well as they would elsewhere. Then again, some golfers will use any excuse for a lousy shot. The water hazard is a popular spot for waterfowl—and for birdwatchers. The Audubon Society has built an observation platform there. All the bird poop has promoted the growth of reeds.

Q. Around 1930 the Borax Company turned its abandoned employee facilities at Ryan, just outside the park boundary, into a tourist lodge. An old "baby gauge" ore railroad, which had tracks two feet (0.6 m) apart, was converted to carry tourists along mountain slopes and through old mine tunnels. Passengers sat on wooden benches wide enough for two people. The train was powered by a Plymouth automobile engine. The conductor loved to joke with tourists. Coming up to one turn, he told them they would soon see "a tin mountain." What did they really see?

A. A huge pile of tin cans discarded by miners. The baby gauge railroad remained a popular ride for over 20 years.

Q. When did first automobile drive into Death Valley?

A. In 1904. It was a one-cylinder Cadillac, owned by a man from Los Angeles, who came to Death Valley to inspect a mining investment. In 1907 the first motorcycle crossed in Death Valley.

Q. In 1908 the world was amazed by "The Great Race," an around-the-world car race that started in New York City, crossed the United States, went through Death Valley to San Francisco, started again on the Pacific coast of Asia, and ended in Paris. Almost the whole race took place on dirt roads—if there were any roads at all. Only three cars made it as far as

---

The restaurant at Stovepipe Wells includes timbers from a borax mine and...

Death Valley. The first to arrive was the American entry in the race, a car called the Thomas Flyer. How long did this car take to go from New York City to Death Valley?

A) 9 days   B) 19 days   C) 39 days

A. C) 39 days, or an average of 80 miles (129 km) per day. A week later the Italian entry reached Death Valley, made a wrong turn, and left Death Valley going the wrong way. Soon the French entry arrived, but in a sandstorm it went off the road, got stuck in the Mesquite Flat Sand Dunes, and needed to be rescued. The Thomas Flyer ended up winning the race.

Q. The Great Race convinced car companies that Death Valley was a great place to test cars, and to advertise them. In 1908 the Packard Company started the tradition—still going strong today—of sending cars to Death Valley to prove they could conquer heat. Five years later a Dodge got stuck in the same sand dunes that had caught the French entry in the Great Race, and this time the driver died. But that didn't stop the Dodge Company from issuing a 1916 booklet called *Through Death Valley in a Dodge Brothers Motor Car*, which boasted that Dodge cars had survived "the most strenuous trip ever recorded in the annals of motoring." The Dodge book claimed the temperature was 144 F (63 C). The Nash Company claimed it had beaten 151 F (66 C). Do you see anything wrong with these claims?

A. The record temperature in Death Valley was "only" 134 F (56.6 C). Advertising has been known to exaggerate.

Q. When you hike up Golden Canyon, you see something odd: long slabs of asphalt, as if there used to be a road here. What is it?

A. There really was a road here, built for tourists in the 1920s. Golden Canyon was a foolish place for a road, not only because it's so narrow, but because it's subject to flash floods. In 1976, a four-day rain dumped 2.3 inches (5.8 cm) of rain in the area and tore apart the Golden Canyon road.

In the 1880s a man named George Albright was working as a miner about 100 miles (161 km) north of Death Valley. His growing family prompted him to go into a new business, along with a partner, Chris Zabriskie, who had been the local

...A meeting room in Furnace Creek Inn includes timbers from a railroad trestle.

Wells Fargo agent. They became undertakers. Their motto was "Albright and Zabriskie. A to Z: You kick the bucket, we do the rest." With a start like this, it seems fitting that the sons of George Albright and Chris Zabriskie went on to play major roles in the history of Death Valley. Horace Albright became the deputy of Stephen Mather, who was the first director of the National Park Service, and in 1929 Albright became the second director of the NPS. Albright oversaw Death Valley becoming a national monument. Christian Zabriskie became a top executive of the Borax Company and helped to develop tourist facilities in Death Valley. Zabriskie Point was named for him.

Q. Which U. S. president created Death Valley National Monument?
A) Teddy Roosevelt B) Herbert Hoover
C) Franklin Roosevelt
A. B) Herbert Hoover created Death Valley National Monument on Feb 11, 1933, with 2 million acres (0.8 million ha). In 1937 Franklin Roosevelt added "the Nevada triangle." In 1952 Harry Truman added Devils Hole to protect its pupfish. In 1994 Bill Clinton signed the California Desert Protection Act, which promoted Death Valley to a national park and expanded it to nearly 3.4 million acres (1.37 million ha).

Q. How many people visited Death Valley National Monument in its first year?
A) 9,970   B) 29,970   C) 129,970
A. A) 9,970. By 1941, Death Valley passed the 100,000 mark. In 1995, the year after Death Valley became a national park, it received over one million visitors.

Q. What percentage of America's national parks were originally national monuments?
A) 5 percent   B) 20 percent   C) Nearly 50 percent
A. C) Nearly 50 percent. Of 58 national parks, 28 started as

Some employee housing at Furnace Creek Ranch was moved from Hoover Dam...

national monuments. A national monument can be created by a presidential proclamation, while a national park requires a vote of Congress. President Teddy Roosevelt created many national monuments, including the Grand Canyon, at a time when Congress often refused to protect natural wonders.

Q. By the time America started creating national parks, much of the West had been claimed by mining companies. The National Park Service often spent decades fighting mining companies for control of claims inside park boundaries. But in two ways, Death Valley was different. The major mining company there, the Borax Company, was actually pushing for the creation of a national monument. The Borax Company was no longer mining inside Death Valley, but other mining companies were still mining there. President Hoover, a former mining engineer, didn't want to interfere with active mines, so he made Death Valley the only national monument or park that allowed mining to continue within park boundaries. In 1976 Congress passed a law eliminating mining inside Death Valley National Monument. But the mine at Ryan, just outside the monument boundary, found a way to get around this law. What did they do?
A. They sank a diagonal shaft under the park boundary to get to ore underneath park lands. This was legal, since the NPS didn't control the ore underground.

Q. Soon after President Hoover created Death Valley National Monument, a new president, Franklin Roosevelt, created a new agency that became very important for Death Valley. The Civilian Conservation Corps (CCC) was a Great Depression program that gave jobs to young men and helped support their families back home. The CCC played a larger role in Death Valley than in other parks or monuments, for as a new monument, Death Valley lacked basic infrastructure. The CCC built roads, wells, water lines, telephone lines, hiking trails, five campgrounds, and 76 buildings, including ranger offices and housing. How many miles of roads were graded by the CCC in Death Valley?
   A) 100 (161 km)   B) 250 (402 km)   C) 500 (804 km)
A. C) The CCC graded 500 miles (804 km) of roads, and paved much of that. The CCC had 1,200 men working in Death Valley.

...where it served as construction-crew housing in the 1930s.

One of their camps is now the Wildrose Campground, which still has the CCC's concrete pads and foundations. Some CCC workers were so inspired by the national parks that they went into careers in the National Park Service, including Granville Liles, who became Superintendent of Death Valley National Monument in the 1960s.

Q. In 1949, Death Valley hosted a celebration for the 100th anniversary of the trek of the Death Valley 49ers. The master of ceremonies was actor James Stewart. Organizers expected maybe 3,000 people, and built a grandstand for 5,000. How many people showed up?

   A) 500   B) 10,000   C) 100,000

A. C) 100,000. Roads were jammed, and stores ran out of food and gas. This event gave birth to the "Death Valley 49ers" organization, whose annual Encampment in November remains one of the largest celebrations in any national park, attracting thousands of people.

Q. Why do inner-city kids in Los Angeles say "Death Valley Rocks!"?

A. "Death Valley R.O.C.K.S." (Recreation Outdoors for Kids Through Study) is a program that brings inner-city kids to Death

Valley to experience a national park. This program was started by Death Valley Superintendent J. T. Reynolds, one of the first African Americans to become superintendent of a major national park (from 2000 to 2008). He realized that, for financial reasons, city kids often had little chance to

A Death Valley R.O.C.K.S. outing

visit a national park. For some kids, visiting and camping in Death Valley changes their lives.

A Wildrose charcoal kiln took one week to produce 2,100 bushels of charcoal.

SCOTTY'S CASTLE
SCOTTY DIDN'T SLEEP HERE,
HE ONLY LIED HERE

Bust of Scotty at the Castle

"A mine is just a hole in the ground owned by a liar."
—Mark Twain

"There's many a good mine that's been spoiled by a pick."
—Death Valley Scotty

Q. Death Valley is an extreme place, and the people who were up to the challenges of living there were often extreme characters—tough, strong-willed, eccentric. The most famous of all Death Valley characters became so identified with Death Valley that he was known as "Death Valley Scotty." Scotty was born in 1872 in Kentucky, and grew up in the years when the western frontier was disappearing and Americans were becoming nostalgic for it. Scotty spent ten years in Buffalo Bill's Wild West Show, where he saw the power of the myth of the West. Americans saw the West as a romantic realm of adventure, freedom, heroes, and quick wealth. Scotty next headed west and tried to wrap himself in this myth. While Scotty was often a cynical con artist, he was also acting out a role that Americans loved. Scotty became famous for having what icon of the Wild West?

A) A huge cattle ranch
B) A gold mine
C) A stage coach line

A. B) A gold mine. Scotty claimed that his gold mine had built Scotty's Castle. In truth, Scotty never had any gold mine. But he did make a friend, Albert Johnson, who loved the myth of the West and was rich enough to build a castle in Death Valley. Albert Johnson was happy to play along with Scotty's claim that his gold mine had paid for the castle.

Q. Scotty used many tricks to get investors to put money into his gold mine, such as showing off gold nuggets he had actually obtained in Colorado. Then Scotty used many tricks to hide the fact that there wasn't any gold mine. When one of Scotty's investors, Albert Johnson, first came out to Death Valley in 1906 to see Scotty's mine, what trick did Scotty use to try to fend off Johnson?

A) He built a fake gold mine.
B) He pretended he was too sick to travel.
C) He staged a fake ambush by robbers.

A. C) He hired people to stage a fake ambush as his group was on its way to his gold mine. But the bullets they were firing were real, and Scotty's brother was wounded, forcing Scotty to call off the attack. Scotty's brother didn't forgive him, but Albert Johnson eventually did.

Albert Johnson had a degree in mining engineering from Cornell University, and he was starting a mining career in the West, but then a Colorado train wreck left him disabled, unable to walk without pain. Johnson was forced to settle for the life of a deskbound Chicago businessman. He had to watch other men—like Scotty—living the venturesome

Scotty's Castle is 3,000 feet (914 m) higher than Furnace Creek, making it cooler too.

Western life he had wanted. When Johnson came out to Death Valley, he discovered that the desert heat helped his health considerably. The combination of health needs and a lingering taste for Wild West adventure prompted Johnson to build his castle in Death Valley. The castle even included a room for Scotty. But Albert and his wife Bessie were an odd match for Scotty. The Johnsons were very religious and didn't approve of cussing, smoking, drinking, or gambling—all of which Scotty indulged in. It helped that Scotty actually lived in his own little place a few miles from the Johnsons; he came to the castle mainly when they had guests who wanted to be entertained with Wild West stories.

Q. If you look closely at Albert Johnson's bookshelves, you can see that they include the works of a famous 1800s novelist. It's very appropriate that this novelist's books are here. Who was he?

    A) Sir Walter Scott   B) Mark Twain   C) Zane Grey

A. A) Sir Walter Scott, the English author of adventure novels like *Ivanhoe*. Death Valley Scotty's real name was Walter Scott—he was named for the novelist Walter Scott. Albert Johnson was captivated by the novelist Walter Scott's romantic adventure stories, which often featured castles. Death Valley Scotty had the perfect name for capturing Johnson's imagination.

Q. To design his Death Valley home, Albert Johnson hired a Chicago architect, but this architect's plans weren't good enough for Johnson, so Johnson fired him. Today this architect is considered the greatest architect in American history. Who was he?

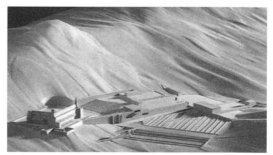
Wright's design

A. Frank Lloyd Wright. Wright's design was too modernistic for Johnson, who decided on a Spanish-style castle.

The spring above Scotty's Castle produces 100 gallons (379 L) of water per minute.

Q. How much did Scotty's Castle cost to build in the 1920s?
  A) $1 million
  B) $2 million
  C) $25 million
A. B) Nearly $2 million. In today's money, that's more like $25 million.

Q. The boundary of Albert Johnson's property was 45 miles (72 km) long. When he fenced it off, how many concrete fence posts did he use?
  A) 4,000   B) 10,000   C) 14,000
A. C) 14,000. Many are still there today.

Q. Surveyors in Death Valley must have flunked their surveying classes. The owners of both Scotty's Castle and the Stovepipe Wells lodge were shocked to discover they had the same problem. What was it?
A. They had built their buildings on land they didn't actually own. The land they did own was a mile (1.6 km) or so away. Their maps had been wrong. Fortunately the National Park Service allowed them to make land swaps. And Albert Johnson got the last laugh. In 1930 he bought land that included Ubehebe Crater, and his heirs quietly paid taxes on it for 30 years. In 1960 the NPS was shocked to discover that it didn't own Ubehebe Crater. The next year, the NPS bought it.

Many of the castle's construction workers were local Native Americans.

Q. Scotty first won national fame in 1909 when he chartered a Santa Fe Railway train that set a speed record between Los Angeles and Chicago. Scotty claimed that the train cost him $100,000. How much did it really cost?

    A) $50,000   B) $25,000   C) $5,500

A. C) $5,500, and it wasn't even Scotty's own money.

Q. When it came to being dishonest, Death Valley Scotty found some famous company. In 1911 Scotty and another man were arrested in Los Angeles for running a crooked gambling game. Who was the other man?

    A) Wyatt Earp   B) Errol Flynn   C) Buffalo Bill

A. A) Wyatt Earp, the famous lawman of Dodge City and Tombstone.

Q. Scotty's Castle has 14 fireplaces, some of them huge. But this was a problem: there's no firewood in the desert. Where did the Johnsons get their firewood?

    A) From the Panamint Mountains   B) Old railroad ties

    C) From the Sierras

A. B) Old railroad ties. At the time the Castle was being built, a nearby railroad was being abandoned. Albert Johnson bought 120,000 wooden ties for $1,500, though it cost him $25,000 to transport them. About 40,000 of those ties are still stacked up in "Tie Canyon" behind the Castle.

Q. One of the highlights of a Scotty's Castle tour is the playing of the 1920s theater organ. In the era of silent movies an organist or pianist played music to liven up a movie, and theaters that were huge needed powerful theater organs. Albert Johnson spent $50,000 to buy, transport, and install his Welte-Mignon organ. How many pipes does the organ have?

    A) 27   B) 501   C) 1,121

A. C) 1,121. The organ required so much electricity that it had to wait for the arrival of the castle's diesel generator. Today the organ plays automatically, but once a year a live organist comes to give a live concert.

Scotty was born in the same small Kentucky town, Cynthiana, as William Coleman, the Borax Company president who built Harmony Borax Works.

Vulture Culture
Death Valley in movies, books, TV, and music

Q. Death Valley has been the location for more Hollywood movies than most national parks, partly because it's one of the closest parks to Hollywood. It's also close to the Alabama Hills (at Lone Pine), one of the most famous settings for western movies. Which Death Valley location has been used for movies most often?
  A) Zabriskie Point   B) Mesquite Flat Sand Dunes   C) Badwater
A. A) The badlands around Zabriskie Point.

Q. What was the first movie filmed in Death Valley?
A. In 1913 a movie company came to Death Valley to film *Life's Whirlpool*, a film version of Frank Norris's famous novel *McTeague*, whose ending takes place in Death Valley. But this film company

didn't come to Death Valley because it was nearby; it was from New Jersey. They were forced to come all the way across the country because Frank Norris's heirs wouldn't allow them to film the book unless it was filmed in Death Valley. Death Valley Scotty served as the film crew's guide. Afterward, the director swore he wouldn't take $10 million to repeat their grueling desert experience. Unfortunately, *Life's Whirlpool* has been lost—no copy survives.

Q. Film historians consider the most legendary of all lost movies to be *Greed*, the next attempt to film *McTeague* in Death Valley. It was filmed in 1923 by eccentric, obsessive director Erich von Stroheim, who today is best remembered for playing the eccentric, former-director-turned-butler in *Sunset Boulevard*. Von Stro-

heim insisted on total realism, which meant filming in 120 F (49 C) summer heat. The actors were soon dehydrated, sunburned, and exhausted. Star Jean Hersholt lost 27 pounds (12 kg) and ended up in the hospital. Von Stroheim described the experience as "in hell, knee deep." He shot 200 rolls of film and couldn't bear to discard his hard work. When he finished editing the movie, how long was it?

A) 5 hours   B) 7 hours   C) 9 hours

A. C) 9 hours. The movie studio forced him to cut it to 3½ hours, and then the studio melted down the discarded film to extract the silver in it—speaking of greed!

> "When I came to the desert sequences which were laid in Death Valley, the company suggested that I'd take them in Oxnard...But having read the marvelous descriptions of the real Death Valley as Frank Norris had depicted it, I knew that Death Valley did not look like Oxnard...I insisted on Death Valley, and Death Valley it was."
>
> —Erich von Stroheim

On the night he died in Paris in 1971 Jim Morrison of The Doors went the see the movie Death Valley...

Q. Frank Norris's 1899 novel *McTeague* is all about greed. The character McTeague is a harmless dentist whose wife wins $5,000 in a lottery and becomes obsessed with money, until McTeague ends up murdering her. McTeague flees into the desert with a mule and the $5,000. He wanders into Death Valley and is overwhelmed by the heat. Finally a pursuer catches McTeague, but the pursuer's horse and water have given out. McTeague's mule eats locoweed and tries to run away, carrying his canteen. They shoot the mule to stop it, but they shoot a hole in the canteen. Then McTeague manages to kill his captor. How does the novel end?

A. Now McTeague is handcuffed to a dead body and without water in the middle of Death Valley. His $5,000 doesn't seem so important now.

> "Before him and upon either side...stretched primordial desolation. League upon league the infinite reaches of dazzling white alkali laid themselves out like an immeasurable scroll unrolled from horizon to horizon; not a bush, not a twig relieved that horrible monotony...McTeague had told himself that the heat upon the lower slopes of the Panamint had been dreadful; here in Death Valley it had become a thing of terror. There was no longer any shadow but his own. He was scorched and parched from head to heel. It seemed to him that the smart of his tortured body could not have been keener if he had been flayed."
>
> —Frank Norris, *McTeague*

Q. It's curious that Frank Norris made his character McTeague a dentist, for 25 years later a real dentist would come to Death Valley and write a famous novel about it. Who was he?

    A) Zane Grey   B) Owen Wister   C) Jack London

A. A) Zane Grey. Grey was a dentist in New York City when he decided to start a new life of adventure in the West. Zane Grey did more than anyone to create the genre of the western novel. Frank Norris was one of Grey's inspirations as a writer.

Q. Zane Grey's Death Valley novel, *Wanderer of the Wasteland*, is similar to *McTeague* in that its hero, Adam Larey, flees into Death Valley after killing someone—his brother. Adam spends 14

...Twenty years later, the sand-dune scene in the movie The Doors *was filmed in Death Valley.*

years wandering, trying to make peace with himself, doing good deeds for others, confronting the harshness of nature, yet finding beauty and peace in it. On the last page of the novel, what does Adam discover?

A) Gold   B) True love   C) His brother wasn't dead after all.

A. C) Adam had only wounded his brother, not killed him. Yet Adam decides that his 14 years of wandering in the desert was worth it after all, for he had found spiritual peace there. In 1924, the year after *Greed* was filmed in Death Valley, *Wanderer of the Wasteland* was filmed there, the first western filmed in Technicolor. It offered the world its first good look at Death Valley. But just like *Life's Whirlpool* and *Greed*, no copies of *Wanderer of the Wasteland* have survived.

Q. *McTeague*, with its theme of greed being punished by Death Valley, may have inspired an episode of *The Twilight Zone* TV show sixty years later. In its first season, *The Twilight Zone* aired the episode "I Shot an Arrow into the Air," about the first American manned space flight, which crashes on a desolate asteroid. The astronauts struggle for survival, wandering across a desert, their canteens nearly empty. They fight and kill one another over the remaining water. When only one astronaut is left, he makes a terrible discovery. What is it?

A. He sees a highway sign pointing to Reno, Nevada. All along, they'd been on Earth. In fact, this episode was filmed in Death Valley, in the badlands around Zabriskie Point.

Q. One of the biggest mysteries of Death Valley movie history is a western called *Real Man's Law*. We don't even know what year it was filmed—just sometime in the 1920s. But we do know who starred in it. He went on to become a star in a very different type of film. Who was he?

A) Boris Karloff   B) Fred Astaire
C) Oliver Hardy

A. C) Oliver Hardy, of Laurel and Hardy comedy fame.

In 1925 Paramount Studios restored the bottle house in Rhyolite...

Q. Which John Wayne movie was filmed in Death Valley?
   A) *True Grit*   B) *3 Godfathers*   C) *Hondo*
A. B) *3 Godfathers*. This 1948 western wasn't your typical John Wayne movie. Wayne plays a robber who flees into the desert to escape a posse. There he finds a stranded wagon, its men dead. Only a pregnant woman has survived, but after giving birth, she dies. John Wayne and his two robber buddies become responsible for taking care of the baby, with little food or water, and they discover that they have tender hearts after all.

Q. While there is plenty of wind in Death Valley, you can't count on it to fit into a filming schedule. When director John Ford needed some heavy winds for a scene in *3 Godfathers* in which John Wayne is stumbling over sand dunes in a raging sandstorm, what did he use?
A. Two large wooden airplane propellers. Filming in Death Valley is tough enough without a sandstorm to dry you out. John Wayne drank gallons of water every day to stay hydrated.

Q. When movies are being filmed in Death Valley, the National Park Service sends a ranger to monitor their activities, making sure they don't damage any natural features. When *3 Godfathers* was being filmed in the Mesquite Flat Sand Dunes, the ranger-monitor was amused when John Wayne tried to squeeze water out of a barrel cactus (which doesn't actually grow there—the cactus were brought in for the movie). The ranger told director John Ford that no one could squeeze water out of a barrel cactus, but Ford never liked being told he couldn't do something, so he found a way to film John Wayne squeezing water from the cactus. What trick did Ford use?
A. John Wayne hid a sponge behind the cactus and squeezed water out of the sponge.

Q. The ranger who monitored *3 Godfathers* liked to write songs and sing them at his evening programs. Only a year later, this ranger had the #1 hit song in America. What song was it?
   A) "This Land is Your Land"
   B) "Ghost Riders in the Sky"
   C) "The Ballad of Davy Crockett"

...for the movie The Air Mail, *starring Douglas Fairbanks Jr.*

A. B) "Ghost Riders in the Sky." The ranger's name was Stan Jones. His song, sung by Burl Ives, stayed on the *Billboard* charts of 1949 for 22 weeks, and became a favorite American ballad. Stan Jones grew up in the Arizona desert, where a hermit once told him that clouds are ghost cowboys who ride the skies herding thunderstorms. Soon after the filming of *3 Godfathers*, Jones was monitoring another western movie, and in the evening he sang his songs to the actors and crew. Movie star Randolph Scott encouraged Jones to go to Los Angeles to show off his songs. After "Ghost Riders in the Sky" became a hit, Jones left Death Valley and became a full-time songwriter. Jones wrote nine songs for John Ford westerns. But Ford was still annoyed at Jones for making him look foolish over the cactus, so he kidded Jones: "Don't write anything about cactus. You don't know a goddamned thing about cactus."

Q. When the movie *Twenty Mule Team* was being filmed in Death Valley in the winter of 1940, star Wallace Beery came down with laryngitis from yelling at the mules in his team-driver role. The script called for Beery to be immersed in the pool at Badwater, but the director worried that Beery might get even sicker. What did they do?
A. They heated a tank of water and poured it into the ground, for Beery to sit in.

Q. Some movies put "Death Valley" into their title and claimed they were filmed in Death Valley, but film historians have determined that they were actually filmed elsewhere. This includes *Saga of Death Valley*, starring Roy Rogers, and *Riders of Death Valley*, starring Tom Mix. What skill provides the quickest way to determine that a movie wasn't filmed in Death Valley?
    A) Research in film history archives   B) Botany
A. B) Botany. A botanist can watch a movie and instantly spot plants that don't occur in Death Valley. Of course, in the case of *Saga of Death Valley*, the big herds of cattle Roy Rogers was herding are a pretty obvious clue too: Death Valley is too barren for ranches.

Most of King Solomon's Mines *(1950) was filmed in Africa...*

Before there was a Gower Gulch in Death Valley, there was a famous Gower Gulch in Hollywood. In fact, Death Valley's Gower Gulch was probably named for the one in Hollywood. Hollywood's Gower Gulch was a section of Gower Street that, in the 1920s, was lined with small, third-rate movie studios, which were called "Poverty Row." Poverty Row studios made lots of westerns, so there were always lots of actors dressed as cowboys hanging out on Gower Street. This gave rise to the nickname "Gower Gulch." Gower Street was named for John Gower, who started a ranch there in 1867. John Gower's grandson, Harry Gower, became an executive with the Borax Company for 50 years, and played a major role in developing tourism in Death Valley. It was Harry Gower who named Death Valley's Gower Gulch.

Q. In 1928 an actress wrote and starred in a hit Broadway play, *Diamond Lil*, based on the life of a Death Valley "lady," Katie Fialla. Katie was known as Diamond Lil for the diamond embedded in her gold-capped tooth. The play *Diamond Lil* got even more publicity when it was declared indecent and its author/actress was arrested on morals charges. Five years later this actress starred in a Hollywood movie version of *Diamond Lil* called *She Done Him Wrong*. Who was she?

   A) Gloria Swanson   B) Mae West
   C) Barbara Stanwyck

A. B) Mae West. *Diamond Lil* made her a major star.

Q. Marlon Brando directed only one movie in his life, a 1961 western called *One-Eyed Jacks*. He also starred in it, as a bank robber. The getaway scene was filmed in the badlands around Zabriskie Point. Brando loved Death Valley so much that he did something special there. What?

   A) He celebrated his 50th birthday there.
   B) He donated $1 million to the park.
   C) After his death, his ashes were scattered in Death Valley.

...but the desert scenes were filmed in Death Valley.

A. C) Brando's ashes were divided between his two favorite places, Tahiti and Death Valley. The exact location remains a secret.

> "Once I bought a new bike, left the highway and rode across Death Valley, racing across the desert as fast as I could. The temperature was at least 115 degrees and the engine gave out...simply died from heat exhaustion. I couldn't restart it and had to walk out several miles. A park ranger told me I had been lucky to survive and pointed out a spot not far from the ranger station where two people not long before had expired..."
>
> —Marlon Brando

Q. When Marlon Brando was growing up in Evanston, Illinois, he became best friends with a neighborhood kid. Years later they became roommates in New York City. Brando encouraged his friend to go into acting, and his friend succeeded, but in very different roles than Brando. Brando became famous as a tough guy, while his friend became famous as a bumbling nerd. When his friend died, Brando kept his friend's cremated ashes for years and directed that they be scattered with his own ashes in Death Valley. Who was Brando's friend?

A) Don Knotts   B) Wally Cox   C) Danny Kaye

A. B) Wally Cox. Cox became famous as "Mr. Peepers" on TV in the 1950s.

Q. Next to westerns, the type of movie most often filmed in Death Valley is science fiction. Death Valley's weird landscapes make good alien planets. As which planet has Death Valley starred most often?

A) Mars   B) Venus   C) Jupiter

A. A) Mars. The first movie to use Death Valley as a Martian landscape was *Rocketship X-M* in 1950. In 1964 came *Robinson Crusoe on Mars*. Both movies tinted the Martian landscape red, long before NASA's Viking spacecraft proved that the landscape of Mars really is red. In 1980 Carl Sagan brought a working model of the Viking lander to Death Valley and pretended Death Valley was Mars for an episode of his *Cosmos* series. In 1983 a group of

---

Escape from Fort Bravo *pretended it was set in Arizona...*

astronomical artists toured Death Valley to use its landscapes as models for alien planets; they named one hill "Mars Hill" for its similarity to Mars. In 1992 Mars Hill was used to test the prototype of a Russian Mars rover. Curiously, the first geologist to do a long-term study of the moving rocks of the Racetrack playa, Robert Sharp, was also a pioneer of Mars geology.

Fans of *Star Wars* can have fun in Death Valley trying to spot the locations where some of the original 1977 *Star Wars* movie was filmed. Most of the movie was filmed in the North African desert, but to finish it off on a nearly-depleted budget, director George Lucas stayed closer to Hollywood—Death Valley.

1. When R2-D2 and C-3PO escape their attacked spaceship and land on a sandy planet to search for Obi-wan Kenobi, where are they?
Answer: The Mesquite Flat Sand Dunes, at least for the final shot when R2-D2 and C-3PO go their separate ways.

2. When R2-D2 is wandering up a narrow canyon and is seized by Jawas, where is he?
Answer: Artists Palette. The Jawas were played by local children.

3. Where is the sand crawler scene?
Answer: Near Artists Palette, on a slope just south of where you turn in to the Artists Palette parking lot.

4. When Luke Skywalker is attacked by the sand people riding the Banta "elephants," where is he?
Answer: Desolation Canyon.

5. When Luke Skywalker and Obi-wan Kenobi look down on the spaceport where they'll find Hans Solo, where are they?
Answer: Dantes View, looking north toward Furnace Creek Ranch.

...but much of it was filmed in Death Valley.

Q. *The Return of the Jedi* also included a scene in Death Valley, though it wasn't filmed there, just imposed as a special effect. It's the scene where R2-D2 and C-3PO go to Jabba's palace. Where is this?
A. 20 Mule Team Canyon.

Q. The opening scenes of the Roman epic *Spartacus* were filmed at the old borax mines at Ryan. What were the Roman slaves do- ing in this scene?
    A) Mining borax   B) Gladiator fighting
    C) Starting a rebellion
A. A) Mining borax. They were even using old ramps left by the borax miners. Since Ryan was outside the park boundary, the pick-swinging actors could dislodge rocks in a way that wouldn't have been allowed inside the park.

Q. True or false: Bette Davis and James Cagney were in a plane crash in Death Valley.
A. True, but only in the movie *The Bride Came C.O.D.* Cagney was kidnapping Davis, but after they crashed in the Mesquite Flat Sand Dunes, they took refuge in a ghost town and ended up falling in love.

Q. *Zabriskie Point* was a 1970 movie named for the popular over- look in Death Valley. As with all movies filmed in Death Valley, the National Park Service assigned a ranger to monitor the filming. But at one point the director lured the monitor into a tent for lunch and hurriedly filmed a scene he didn't want the monitor to see. What was so secret about this scene?
A. It was a nude scene. It wasn't much fun for the actors who had to lie naked on the rough desert ground.

Q. *Death Valley Days* originated as a radio show, which aired from 1930 to 1945. It was sponsored by the Borax Company to promote its soap products. All of the scripts for the radio show were written by Ruth Cornwall Woodman. When she was hired, she had never even been to the West. She began making an annual trip west to talk with old miners and get ideas for the show. How many scripts did she write for *Death Valley Days*?

The Death Valley scene in Anne Rice's Queen of the Damned...

A) 320   B) 520   C) 720

A. C) 720. When *Death Valley Days* became a TV show, Woodman helped convert many radio scripts for TV.

Stanley Andrews

Q. The *Death Valley Days* television show was hosted by "the old ranger," who introduced the stories and promoted borax soap. For the first dozen years "the old ranger" was Stanley Andrews. He was replaced by an actor whose movie career was pretty much washed up. This host lasted only one season, though he also guest-starred in eight *Death Valley Days* episodes that season. Then he quit to seek a better job. What job did he find?

A. Governor of California. The actor was Ronald Reagan. Fourteen years after hosting *Death Valley Days*, Reagan was elected president of the United States.

Q. When the crew of the original *Star Trek* TV show landed on a desert planet, three of its actors may have felt right at home. Why was this?

   A) They liked to vacation in Death Valley.

   B) They had made guest appearances on *Death Valley Days*.

A. B) Leonard Nimoy (Spock) and George Takei (Sulu) each made one guest appearance on *Death Valley Days* in 1965, and DeForest Kelley (Dr. McCoy) made four guest appearances between 1962 and 1966.

Q. What future star of TV and movie westerns got a break with a guest appearance on *Death Valley Days* in 1956, at age 26? (Hint: it "made his day.")

A. Clint Eastwood. Eastwood played a prospector who was so discouraged he was ready to commit suicide, when he got a letter saying he'd inherited a family fortune. Ironically, as an actor Eastwood was so discouraged he was ready to quit, and this role helped keep him going.

...was actually filmed in Australia.

For Easter in 1938, poet Robinson Jeffers was supposed to fly to Death Valley with his brother, a private pilot. Jeffers had a premonition that their plane would crash along the way. Jeffers wrote a long letter to his wife and left it atop his desk, spelling out his wishes for his funeral. Jeffers reached Death Valley safely, had a good visit, returned home safely, and threw the letter away.

Q. Dantes View was named for:
   A) An NFL quarterback
   B) An Italian poet
   C) A surrealistic artist

A. B) Dantes View was named for poet Alighieri Dante, who wrote *The Divine Comedy*, one of the masterpieces of world literature. The first part of it, "The Inferno," relates Dante's journey through all the layers of Hell.

Q. If you were standing at Badwater on the night of May 29, 1947, you would have seen someone up at Dantes View using a high-intensity searchlight to sweep the floor of Death Valley. Who was it?
   A) An idiot who didn't appreciate nature
   B) A ranger searching for a lost hiker
   C) A world-famous nature photographer

A. C) It was Ansel Adams, America's most famous nature photographer. Adams was a leader of the Sierra Club, dedicated to protecting nature from human intrusions. But this couldn't stop Adams from indulging his photographer's passion for seeing nature in every kind of light.

Q. Edward Weston was one of the most famous photographers of the 20th century. He loved to photograph Death Valley, but found it a tough place for a photographer. The sun went right through the black cloth he used for covering his head to focus his camera, leaving him badly sunburned. He switched to a white cloth, and painted his equipment boxes white to protect his camera and film. Weston was especially fascinated by what he called "the Athens of the West." What was this?

The ghost town of Rhyolite includes a sculpture garden of ghost sculptures...

A. The ghost town of Rhyolite, whose ruined arches and columns reminded Weston of the Acropolis.

> When Americans first encountered Death Valley and the rest of the desert Southwest, they seldom regarded it as beautiful. Their idea of beauty came from England, a beauty of green hills and blue lakes. But a few visionary American writers decided that the desert held a deep beauty of its own. They were nature writers, who use personal experiences and poetic prose to explore landscapes. John C. Van Dyke was a Rutgers art professor who moved to the Mojave Desert in 1898 to seek a cure for severe asthma. He decided that the desert was better than any art gallery. He roamed the Mojave Desert and published his experiences in *The Desert* in 1901. Two years later Mary Austin, who lived in Independence just west of Death Valley, published *Land of Little Rain*. The best book focused largely on Death Valley is *The White Heart of Mojave* by Edna Brush Perkins. In 1920 Perkins tried to explore Death Valley by car, only to retreat and try again by horse and wagon. Perkins's book is partly a rugged adventure story, but it soon becomes a poetic and spiritual adventure, about testing of the meanings of life against a landscape of death.

Q. The same American composer who wrote "Grand Canyon Suite" (with its famous clip-clopping of mules on the trail) also wrote a "Death Valley Suite." Who was he?

    A) Ferde Grofe   B) George Gershwin   C) Aaron Copland

A. A) Ferde Grofe. "Death Valley Suite" received its world premiere at the 49ers centennial celebration in 1949 in Death Valley, and was performed by the Hollywood Bowl Orchestra.

> Because of a flat tire, there's a famous opera house just outside Death Valley. Marta Beckett grew up in the artistic world of New York City, and danced in Broadway shows like *Showboat*. In the 1950s she developed a solo dance-and-mime act and toured the country with it. During a break in 1967 she visited Death Valley. When she got a flat tire, she was told that the only place to get it fixed was in Death Val-

---

...made by draping plaster-soaked burlap over live models.

ley Junction, a dusty little town outside Death Valley. There, Beckett found an abandoned Spanish-style building with a long colonnade and courtyard—and a theater. This complex had been built by the Borax Company in 1924 as a headquarters and employee quarters. Around 1920 Zane Grey visited Death Valley Junction and saw the workers living in shabby conditions, and he wrote about it in a national magazine. In response, the Borax Company decided to build something it could be proud of. When Marta Beckett saw the theater, it was in terrible shape, with a leaking roof, and full of debris. But she fell in love with the idea of having her own little theater. She fixed it up, painted it with murals, and put on her first show in 1968—with an audience of twelve. Many people told Marta she was crazy. But the Amargosa Opera House became a legend, and Beckett was still going strong four decades later.

The first tour buses in Death Valley were loaned from Zion and Bryce National Parks, where they weren't needed in winter.

DEATH IN
DEATH VALLEY

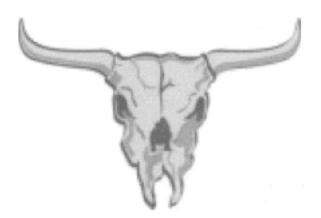

Q. How many people have died unnaturally in Death Valley?
  A) 40   B) 200   C) 1,200
A. B) Since 1849, about 200 people have died unnaturally in Death Valley. The count is a bit uncertain, since in prospecting days no one was keeping count, and many prospectors simply disappeared in the desert.

Q. In prospecting days, what was the leading cause of death?
  A) Heat and dehydration   B) Mine cave-ins   C) Murders
A. A) Heat and dehydration.

Q. What was the deadliest year in Death Valley?
A. In 1905, the height of the Bullfrog gold rush, 13 people are known to have died in or near Death Valley. People were buried wherever they were found. But there was little wood for grave markers. One grave was marked by an ironing board.

> "From end to end Death Valley is strewn with leaching, sun-dried, vulture-picked skeletons."
> —*Wilmington* (Ohio) *Journal*, 1905

Q. What causes the most deaths today?
A) Heat and dehydration   B) Car wrecks   C) Rattlesnakes
A. B) Car wrecks. These are mostly single-vehicle wrecks, one car going off the road and crashing into boulders or rolling over. Since all the passes into Death Valley are 3,000 feet (914 m) or higher and the descent is often steep, cars easily gain too much speed and wipe out on a curve. In summer, brakes overheat. Even on flat, straight highways, drivers get impatient, go too fast, and veer off the road.

Q. How many people are known to have died of rattlesnake bites in Death Valley?
A) Zero   B) 13   C) 127
A. A) Zero. The floor of Death Valley is too hot and dry even for most rattlesnakes. Prospectors said that if you put a rattlesnake in a bucket in the summer heat, it would die within 20 minutes. Also there isn't much prey—like mice—for rattlesnakes.

Q. How many people are known to have been bitten by rattlesnakes in Death Valley?
A) 3   B) 33   C) 133
A. A) Only 3. Rattlesnakes are not only rare, they spend a lot of time hiding from the sun, which keeps them safely out of the way of people. One of those three bites occurred when a boy was playing in the Mesquite Flat Sand Dunes and stuck his arm into a burrow in the side of a dune—guess whose home it was? Another

Prospectors believed that the floor of Death Valley was full of poison gas...

bite happened to a guy who had seen a TV show about preachers who pick up rattlesnakes as a test of faith; in his case, it was only a test of his foolishness.

Q. How many people are known to have died from scorpion bites in Death Valley?

   A) Zero   B) 23   C) 57

A. A) Zero. The scorpions in Death Valley, which are up to six inches (15 cm) long, may look scary, and their stings are painful, but their venom isn't strong enough to kill humans.

Q. How did the Keane Wonder Mine kill one tourist?

   A) It caved in.   B) Poison gases   C) He fell down a shaft.

A. C) He walked into a tunnel, without a flashlight, stepped into a vertical shaft, and fell 20 feet (6 m) to his death. He also ignored all the warning signs placed by the National Park Service. The NPS doesn't have the resources to close off all the old mines in Death Valley; it has to rely on the common sense of tourists.

Q. Death Valley's heat has more than one trick for claiming lives. Prospectors sometimes died of thirst even when they had a full canteen. What happened?

A. The water in canteens, especially metal canteens, became too hot to drink.

Q. Over the decades there have been a number of reports of heat-dazed people wandering naked in Death Valley, holding their clothes in the air above their heads. Why were they doing this?

   A) To keep their clothes dry from floodwaters

   B) To signal for help

   C) To shade themselves

A. A) When questioned, victims seemed to think they were drowning, and they were holding up their clothes to keep them dry—though there was no water. This seems to be a delusion brought on by extreme thirst.

Q. The National Park Service often receives packages from people who are returning things they removed—illegally—from national parks, things like arrowheads, petrified wood, or Civil War bullets.

...they couldn't believe that the valley's death toll was caused by heat alone.

Often, people report that stealing this object brought on a curse, a run of bad luck. In 1953, in 112 F (44 C) heat, two youths drove to a Death Valley canyon to collect rocks for their rock collection. What "curse" befell them?

A. Their vehicle got stuck in the gravel. Within only a jug of lemonade to drink, they tried to hike 14 miles (22 km) back to Furnace Creek in the afternoon heat. Both died.

Q. In 1991 a young man impulsively decided to hike cross-country, alone, from Badwater to the top of Telescope Peak. Tricked by Death Valley's lack of perspective, he completely underestimated the distance. He carried an impossibly small amount of water. Before he had crossed the salt pan, he realized he was in trouble and turned back. He made it to within a few hundred feet of his car, then collapsed and died. It took rangers two weeks to find him. We know everything this victim did and said and suffered on his ordeal. How do we know this?
A. He videotaped the whole ordeal. The camera was still running when he collapsed.

Q. True or false: Blizzards kill people in Death Valley.
A. True. On Thanksgiving Day in 1960 a 17-year-old youth decided to climb Telescope Peak, but a blizzard caught him. When he failed to return, rangers searched for him for five days. When the snows melted in the spring, they searched again, and they found where he had fallen down a slope and smashed his skull on a sharp rock.

Q. Some people imagine that if they get in trouble in Death Valley, rangers will come and find them. One time, two soldiers from Ft. Irwin were exploring Death Valley by jeep when they ran out of gas and tried to walk out. How many soldiers came to search for them, and for how long?
   A) 20 soldiers for 2 days   B) 200 soldiers for 4 days
   C) 2,000 soldiers for a week
A. C) 2,000 soldiers searched for them for a week. They found one body, severely dehydrated, but never found the other body. Undoubtedly, Death Valley holds many undiscovered skeletons. In

Death Valley and the arctic are very similar...

1996 rangers found the abandoned van of four German tourists, stuck on a rock. Their skeletons weren't found until 13 years later.

Q. When prospectors perished in the desert, their burros sometimes found their way to distant springs. But when Death Valley pioneer Jimmy Dayton perished in 1899, his four horses died too. What happened to them?
A. Dayton had tied them up, so they couldn't get away. But when searchers found Dayton's body, his dog was still alive, still guarding him. Bite marks on the dog indicated that he had fought off coyotes.

Q. If coyotes or other animals don't get to a dead body, what happens to it in Death Valley?
A. It mummifies, drying out until the skin is like dark leather.

In Death Valley, death comes in many forms:

In July, 1973, two young men set off to hike across the Badwater salt pan, a 12-mile (19 km) roundtrip. They wore no hats or shirts. When one youth fainted from the heat, his friend tried to carry him out, then abandoned him where he died.

One man tried to hike across the Badwater salt pan in 120 F (49 C) heat. It took rangers three days to find him. He had veered off course, aiming miles away from where he had parked his car. He had probably become too delusional to find his way.

In July, 1971, a 23-year-old theology student came to Death Valley on a private religious pilgrimage. Intending to fast, he set off walking across Death Valley without food or water, only a Bible. It took a helicopter to find his body.

A former mental patient declared that his horoscope said that his time to die had come. He set out walking across Death Valley. His death was ruled a suicide.

*...they both preserve dead bodies, one by drying,
the other by freezing.*

Q. Do people come to Death Valley to commit suicide?
A. Occasionally. Some people are attracted by the name "Death Valley." For others, Death Valley has personal meaning. Botanists Al and Lynn Kichner had done extensive botanical work in Death Valley. When Lynn died, Al didn't want to go on living without her, and came to Death Valley to die.

> Like many Death Valley boomtowns, Greenwater had a lively saloon scene. When the printer of the local newspaper died and was laid out in his coffin, Diamond Lil decided that "He just doesn't look quite natural." She placed five cards—all aces—in his right hand over his chest. He was buried that way.

Q. A famous murderer and his gang hid out in an abandoned ranch just outside of Death Valley. Who was he?
   A) Jesse James   B) Charles Manson   C) John Dillinger
A. B) Charles Manson. In the late 1960s Manson's cult-like "family" occupied the Barker Ranch in the Panamint Mountains a few miles outside the park boundary. Manson believed that there was an underground paradise beneath Death Valley and spent days searching for the secret entrance. After committing his murders in Los Angeles, Manson fled to the Barker Ranch, and it was here he was arrested, with the help of Death Valley NPS rangers.

> "Tom was buried on a mesa above Salt Creek, but that was not the end of his story. He kept 'coming up.' The wind took special delight in blowing the sand off his shallow grave until it became the regular, the customary, the polite, the expected thing for anyone who passed that way to carry a shovel and throw a few spadefuls of sand over him again."
> —Dr. Margaret Long, *The Shadow of the Arrow*

Q. True or false: A Death Valley murderer was lynched, buried, then dug up from the grave and hung a second time.
A. False. Like a lot of Death Valley legends, this widespread legend has gotten a bit out of hand. In 1908 Hootch Simpson killed a popular citizen of Skidoo on Easter, and the victim's friends lynched Hootch from a telephone pole. The next morning the

In the record-setting heat of 1913, Peter Busch's car bogged down in sand...

local doctor, wanting to make a full report to the sheriff, had Simpson's corpse—still bearing its hanging rope—re-hanged from the rafters of the hospital tent, and the doctor took a photo of it. This photo eventually got published, and it led to the legend that a *Los Angeles Times* reporter had showed up in Skidoo soon after the lynching and cajoled someone into digging up Hootch and re-hanging him so the reporter could take a photograph.

Q. In 1890, prospector Mike Lane came upon a dead man lying in the desert, and buried him. Lane never forgot the dead man's face, since the dead man was almost the only African American

he'd ever seen in the Mojave Desert. Eighteen years later Lane was in Rhyolite and was shocked to recognize—walking down the street!—the black man he'd buried long ago. Lane, himself pale as a ghost, went up to the man and asked him if he was a ghost. What did the "ghost" say?

A. The man recalled how many years before he must have fainted from the heat, and the next thing he knew, he was waking up beneath a shallow pile of sand and brush—maybe the shade had helped to revive him. He dug himself out. In the rocky desert, Lane hadn't been able to dig a deep grave. The "dead" man, who was now a barber in Rhyolite, asked Lane what had happened to the $18 he'd had in his pocket when he'd "died." Lane paid him back.

As a final word, there's silence, the deep silence of the desert. Like its view of the Milky Way, Death Valley's silence is deeper than anywhere else. For some people, this is "the silence of the grave." Zane Grey remarked: "How deep the silence! Dead, vast, sepulcher-like...This silence had something terrifying in it." Frank Norris's McTeague heard: "Not a twig rattled, not an insect hummed, not a bird or beast invaded that huge solitude with call or cry." Even a nature lover like Edna Brush Perkins was troubled: "It was the far-spread, motionless silence of the last days when the whole earth will be dying." Yet Father John J. Crowley heard a deep peace: "Telescope [Peak] grows rose-colored in the

...he tried to walk out, but died of the heat.

alpenglow, and silence descends upon the desert...Someone remarks: 'Hear that silence.' It is true; the quiet is almost audible." Mary Austin saw beauty: "For all the toll the desert takes of a man it gives compensations, deep breaths, deep sleep, and the communion of the stars."

Rumors have persisted for decades that Charles Manson buried more murder victims near his Death Valley hang-out.

ABOUT THE AUTHOR

Don Lago is the author of *Grand Canyon Trivia* (also published by Riverbend Publishing), the result of many years of exploring the Grand Canyon as a hiker, a kayaker, and a historian. His first visit to a national park was to Yosemite at age four, although his main memory of that visit is the Yogi Bear coin bank he bought there. Since then, his appreciation of national parks has only increased. He has been exploring the national parks of the Southwest for 25 years. He thinks that Death Valley National Park should win the award for the "most surprising" national park. "Many people," he says, "think of Death Valley as only a wide, desolate valley, but it is full of surprises, of fantastic beauty and geology, of great hikes in unique side canyons. For history lovers, Death Valley has a wilder cast of Wild West characters than just about any national park. For movie lovers, Death Valley is the best park for seeing film locations." Lago is well-known for his writings on nature, history, and astronomy, which have appeared for many years in magazines such as *Orion, Astronomy,* and *Air and Space Smithsonian;* he has published several other books.

Q. Where can you answers to hundreds of questions about your favorite national parks?
A. In the National Park Trivia Series!